Study Guid

The Culinary Professional

Joan E. Lewis
Instructional Materials Author
Bloomington, Indiana

Text by
John Draz, CEC, CCE
Christopher Koetke, MBA, CEC, CCE

Publisher
The Goodheart-Willcox Company, Inc.
Tinley Park, Illinois
www.g-w.com

Introduction

The *Study Guide* is designed for use with the text *The Culinary Professional*. As you complete the activities in this *Study Guide*, you review the vocabulary, techniques, tools, and ingredients presented in the text. There are also activities to reinforce the math skills that will help you succeed in the culinary field.

The activities in this study guide are divided into chapters that correspond to those in the text. By reading the text first, you will have the information needed to complete the activities. Try to complete them without referring to the text. Later, you can check the text to complete any answer you did not finish. At that time, you can also compare your answers to the information in the text.

Contents

8

Welcome to the Foodservice Industry

Culinary Terminology

Name _____

Date _____ Period_____

Match the following terms and identifying phrases.

_____ 1. New practices or conditions that point to the way things will be in the future.

_____ 2. Foods grown without synthetic fertilizers or pesticides and from animals that have not received antibiotics or hormones.

_____ 3. The business of making and serving prepared food and drink.

_____ 4. Refers to matters related to the preparation or cooking of food.

_____ 5. Products and practices that can be produced or carried out over a long period of time without a negative effect on the environment.

_____ 6. Welcoming guests and satisfying their needs.

_____ 7. The French word for "kitchen." In the English language, it means a style of cooking.

_____ 8. Meals that are consumed at home but professionally prepared elsewhere.

_____ 9. Rate of pay that allows someone working full-time to support his or her family above the poverty level.

_____ 10. A term for a cook or someone who prepares food.

A. cuisine

B. culinarian

C. culinary

D. foodservice

E. home meal replacement

F. hospitality

G. living wage

H. organic foods

I. sustainable products and practices

J. trends

Using Math to Define the Foodservice Industry

Chapter 1

Activity B

Name _____

Date _____ Period _____

The foodservice industry is so large that it is difficult to grasp. One way to better understand its scope is to think of some of its descriptive statistics in mathematical terms.

A. Estimating output

When you know quantity of output for one time period, you can estimate quantity of output for another time period by multiplication or division. For example, if you know the rate of output for one hour, you could estimate output for an 8-hour day by multiplying the hourly rate by 8. Use this math principle to answer problems 1–3 about the following statistic:

The National Restaurant Association reports that foodservice operations sell over $1.5 billion in meals, snacks, and beverages each day.

1. Estimate the amount of dollars in sales that foodservice operations generate per week.

   _____

   _____

2. Estimate the amount of dollars in sales that foodservice operations generate per month (consider a month to be 30 days).

   _____

   _____

3. Estimate the amount of dollars in sales that foodservice operations generate per year.

   _____

   _____

B. Graphing statistics

4. One way to get a clearer picture of what statistics are describing is to create a graph. In the space to the right, create a circle graph to show that 27 percent of adults had their first work experience in restaurants. Be sure to label the parts of your graph.

(Continued)

Activity B *(Continued)*   **Name** _____

C. Calculating percent change

Calculating the percent increase or decrease offers another way to evaluate data. To calculate percent increase or decrease, follow these steps:

> **Step 1.** Calculate the difference between the two amounts.
>
> **Step 2.** Identify the original amount.
>
> **Step 3.** Substitute these numeric values into this formula: difference ÷ original = decimal
>
> **Step 4.** Multiply the decimal by 100 and add percent sign.

Example: The number of customers increased from 20 to 25. What was the percent increase in customers?

> **Step 1.** Difference is 25 - 20 = 5
>
> **Step 2.** Original amount is 20
>
> **Step 3.** 5 ÷ 20 = 0.25
>
> **Step 4.** 0.25 x 100 = 25% increase in customers

5. The foodservice industry is projected to grow from 13 to nearly 15 million employees between 2007 and 2017. Calculate the percent increase. _____

_____

_____

Reviewing Key Concepts

Chapter 1   **Name** _____

Activity C   **Date** _____ **Period** _____

Part 1: Trends in Foodservice

Read the following descriptions of current trends in foodservice. Complete each paragraph by writing the foodservice trend to which the paragraph refers on the space provided.

1. Foodservice professionals must be able to use spreadsheets and word processing because these are essential tools for management and communications. Advances in cooking equipment allow food to be cooked faster and better than before. New kitchen equipment is making dramatic changes in the way work is done. Tedious tasks are reduced. These developments are bringing about support for more

   _____ _____.

2. More people are working outside the home and working longer hours. Busy lifestyles leave many people with no time to prepare their own food. These changes are supporting the increase in number of foodservice operations that offer

   _____ _____ _____.

3. Through travel and the media, diners are more and more exposed to an ever-widening array of dishes from around the world. Restaurateurs and chefs are constantly exploring the world of food for new items to put on their menus. These practices help promote the

   _____ of _____.

4. The foodservice industry is concerned about the environment. There is a growing interest in utilizing products and practices that can be produced or carried out over a long period of time without a negative effect on the environment. These interests encourage the use of

   _____ _____.

Part 2: Challenges to the Foodservice Industry

Recognizing challenges is the first step in finding solutions. Check each of the following statements that are currently considered challenges for the foodservice industry.

_____   5. Creating enough jobs to supply all the trained workers.

_____   6. Finding enough trained workers to fill all the jobs.

_____   7. Finding ways to pay higher wages and still meet customers' demands for lower prices.

_____   8. Finding ways to lower the minimum wage established by federal law.

_____   9. Meeting the demands for healthier menu options.

_____   10. Producing food that is both satisfying and healthy.

_____   11. Determining chefs' and restaurateurs' responsibility for the health of their guests.

(Continued)

Activity C *(Continued)*   **Name** _____

Part 3: The Culinary Profession

Read each statement below. Circle the letter *T* if the statement is true. If the statement is false, circle *F* and write the corrected statement on the lines that follow.

T   F   12. The essential mission for culinarians is to prepare safe and satisfying food for guests.

_____

_____

T   F   13. People who typically seek to improve and grow find the culinary profession boring.

_____

_____

T   F   14. It is necessary for chefs to know how to prepare food from all cuisines.

_____

_____

T   F   15. The job of a culinary professional comes with great physical demands.

_____

_____

T   F   16. Hours of work for culinary jobs are typically short because the work is centered on mealtimes.

_____

_____

Notes

Understanding Foodservice Operations

Culinary Terminology

Name _____

Date _____ Period _____

Circle the clue in parentheses that best completes each of the following statements.

1. The term (**full-service restaurant**) (**chain restaurant**) (**franchise restaurant**) refers to a restaurant that is part of a group of restaurants owned by the same company.

2. A (**full-service restaurant**) (**chain restaurant**) (**franchise restaurant**) is characterized by employing servers to take the customers' orders and bring the meals to their tables.

3. A business in which only one person owns and often operates the business is a (**partnership**) (**sole proprietorship**) (**franchise**).

4. Catering is (**providing food and service for groups**) (**operating the business on your own**) (**being part of a large company**).

5. A (**partnership**) (**corporation**) (**sole proprietorship**) is granted a charter from the state, which recognizes it as a separate entity with legal rights.

6. An entrepreneur is (**a business in which one person owns and often operates the business**) (**a business with a charter from the state**) (**a person who organizes a business and assumes all the risk for it**).

7. Franchise restaurants are (**operated by one person**) (**part of a larger restaurant chain, but are independently owned**) (**all owned by the same company**).

8. A (**partnership**) (**corporation**) (**sole proprietorship**) is a business in which ownership is shared by two or more people.

9. Institutional foodservice (**employs servers to take orders and bring the meals to the tables**) (**supplies meals for businesses and organizations**) (**requires a charter from the state**).

Identifying Foodservice Establishment Options

Chapter 2

Activity B

Name _____

Date _____Period_____

Complete the organizational chart showing the various types of foodservice establishments that employ chefs and cooks. Fill in each numbered shape with a term or phrase from the following list.

Banquet facilities

Business and organization locations

Clubs

Fine dining

Hotels

Off-premise catering

Private banquet facilities

Quick service

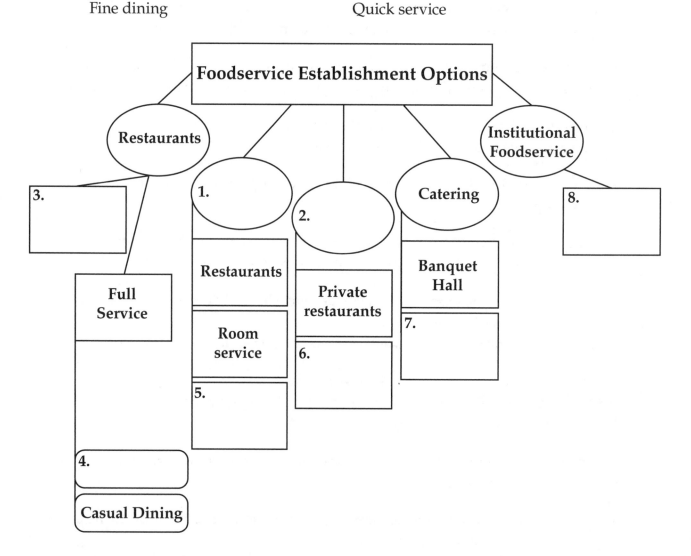

Reviewing Key Concepts

Chapter 2

Activity C

Name _____

Date _____ Period_____

Part 1: Forms of Business Ownership

Foodservice operations, like any business, can take different forms of ownership. The three main legal categories of ownership are *sole proprietorship, partnership,* and *corporation.* Write the category of ownership that best matches each description.

Description   Category of Ownership

1. A business that is owned equally by three people.   _____

2. A business that has been granted a charter from the state.   _____

3. A business that has shareholders who are not responsible for debts of the business.   _____

4. A business that is owned by one person who also operates the business.   _____

5. Legally, this business agreement ends if one of the four owners dies or leaves the business.   _____

6. In this business, one person has final authority on all decisions.   _____

7. A business that has most of the rights and responsibilities of a real person.   _____

8. This business will continue even if one of the several owners dies or leaves.   _____

9. The single owner is personally responsible for all debts of this business.   _____

10. The two owners of this business are each personally responsible for all the debts of the business.   _____

(Continued)

Activity C *(Continued)*   **Name** _____

Part 2: Ways to Organize Foodservice Businesses

Foodservice businesses can be organized in three major ways: independent, chain, and franchise. Various characteristics of foodservice business organizations are listed in this activity. In the space at the left, write *independent, chain,* or *franchise* to indicate the type of foodservice business organization that is described.

_____ 11. Often referred to as "multi-unit foodservice operations."

_____ 12. Can quickly adapt to meet the needs of the guests.

_____ 13. Their size allows them to buy products more cheaply than a single restaurant.

_____ 14. Are independently owned but part of a large group of restaurants.

_____ 15. The owner pays for the right to use the brand name, concept, logo, and advertising of the original company.

_____ 16. Outback Steakhouse restaurant is an example of this type of organization.

_____ 17. McDonald's restaurant is an example of this type of organization.

_____ 18. Is a unique operation.

_____ 19. Have difficulty implementing changes because there are multiple units.

_____ 20. Work hard to make the food and service consistent among all their units.

Part 3: The Risks and Rewards of Entrepreneurship

An entrepreneur is someone who organizes a business and assumes the risk for it. There are risks and rewards of entrepreneurship. Describe the main types of risks and rewards to consider before becoming an entrepreneur.

21. Main type of risk: _____

_____

22. Main type of reward: _____

_____

Workstations in the Professional Kitchen

Brigade Terminology

Chapter 3

Activity A

Name _____

Date _____ Period_____

Match the following terms and identifying phrases.

Part 1

A. baker

B. butcher

C. chef de partie

D. communard

E. entremetier

F. expeditor

G. garde manger

H. pastry chef

I. poissonier

J. potager

K. saucier

L. tournant

_____ 1. Prepares all fish and shellfish items.

_____ 2. Is in charge of the cold food station. Makes salads, dressing, fruit plates, and other cold preparations.

_____ 3. The title used for someone who is in charge of a particular workstation in the kitchen.

_____ 4. Also called the *swing chef* or *roundsman*, this position fills in for other staff members on their days off.

_____ 5. Cuts and trims meats and poultry for other stations in the kitchen.

_____ 6. The head of the baking and pastry department who oversees the work of specialists in that station.

_____ 7. Oversees the preparation and cooking of vegetables, starches, egg dishes, and hot appetizers.

_____ 8. Reads the servers' food orders to the cooks and organizes the finished dishes so servers can deliver them promptly.

_____ 9. Is responsible for making sauces.

_____ 10. Makes all stocks, soups, and mother sauces.

_____ 11. Makes breads and may also make breakfast pastries.

_____ 12. Is responsible for preparing meals for the staff in large operations.

(Continued)

Activity A *(Continued)*   **Name** _____

Part 2

_____ 13. Supervises all the positions in the kitchen, and is responsible for the quality of the food and the safety of the guests and cooks.

_____ 14. Prepares and cooks deep-fried items.

_____ 15. The night chef who is in charge of the kitchen after the chef has left for the evening.

_____ 16. The second in command who assumes the authority and responsibility of the chef when the chef is absent.

_____ 17. Decorates cakes and pastries and makes chocolate carvings or sugar sculptures for pastry displays.

_____ 18. Cooks all grilled and broiled meats, poultry, and fish.

_____ 19. Prepares primarily sweets and pastries.

_____ 20. In charge of roasting meats and poultry and preparing pan sauces or gravies.

_____ 21. Prepares and cooks vegetables.

_____ 22. Assistants in various departments.

A. chef de cuisine

B. chef de garde

C. commis

D. decorator

E. fry cook

F. grill cook

G. légumier

H. pastry cook

I. rotisseur

J. sous chef

Modern Kitchen Organization

Chapter 3

Activity B

Name _____

Date _____ Period_____

Professional kitchens of a hundred years ago required larger staffs than are needed today. Show your understanding of the factors that influence modern kitchen staff organization by answering the following questions.

1. What three factors contribute to the reduced need for staff in the modern kitchen? Consider operation size, technology, and menu.

   _____

   _____

   _____

2. What is the most important factor for determining the staff size and organization of a modern kitchen?

   _____

3. What is the title of the person hired by hotels or resorts to coordinate the operation of their restaurants and departments?

   _____

4. What is the title of the person hired by many hotels to head a special department that prepares meals for large groups?

   _____

5. Traditional kitchens created specialists. When a specialist was absent, it was a problem. How does the modern kitchen use cross training to solve that problem?

   _____

   _____

6. What are three advantages of cross training? Consider scheduling, absenteeism, and job satisfaction.

   _____

   _____

   _____

   _____

Reviewing Key Concepts

Chapter 3

Activity C

Name _____

Date _____ Period _____

Part 1: Working with Other Departments

In large foodservice operations, the kitchen works with other departments. Each department has specific responsibilities. Determine which department is responsible for each of the tasks listed. Below, write the letter of each task in the box under the department that is responsible for it.

Departments Beyond the Kitchen				
Catering	**Dining Room**	**Purchasing**	**Room Service**	**Stewarding**

Tasks

A. Bring foodservice orders to guests' rooms

B. Clean the kitchen

C. Ensure the right products and correct quantities are being purchased

D. Issue goods and supplies out of the storeroom to the cooks as needed

E. Plan banquets

F. Plan catered events

G. Serve the food

H. Store, inventory, and transport serviceware

I. Warewashing

J. Wash pots and pans

(Continued)

Activity C *(Continued)*   **Name** _____

Part 2: Trends in Foodservice to Reduce Labor

Labor is one of the largest costs in the foodservice industry. Advances in foodservice equipment technology have helped reduce the staff size in commercial kitchens. Explain how each of the following pieces of equipment reduces labor needs in the kitchen.

1. Food processors and grinders: _____

   _____

2. Roll-in-rack ovens: _____

   _____

3. Machines that vacuum-pack prepared food: _____

   _____

Many prepared food products, such as pre-cut vegetables, prepared sauces, and frozen pre-cooked meats and vegetables are used in modern kitchens. These products cost more than the basic ingredients needed to make the item.

4. Why do chefs choose these products? _____

   _____

The Professional Chef

Culinary Terminology

Name _____

Date _____Period_____ ____

The following is a professional chef's reply to a student considering a culinary career. Fill in each blank with the appropriate term from Chapter 4. For each term, underline the words in the letter that define that term.

Dear Culinary Hopeful:

To be successful in any field, you need to get specific education and training. In the culinary profession, the standards for your education and training are determined by the 1. _____ _____ _____. It is the largest professional organization for culinarians in the United States. In addition to a great deal of classroom work, you will be required to complete an 2. _____. This is a method of training in which a person learns a trade under the guidance of skilled tradespeople. When you successfully complete this part of your training and pass the test, you will receive the first level of professional 3. _____, which confirms that a culinarian possesses certain knowledge, skill level, and experience.

Be aware that in addition to their culinary knowledge and skills, culinarians are judged for their display of 4. _____. This term refers to the positive behaviors and appearance exhibited by an individual who is committed to the culinary arts. Especially important is how you think and feel about other people and situations—in other words, your 5. _____. You need to work at having a positive outlook.

I find being a professional chef very rewarding, but I would be negligent if I didn't tell you that external pressures, such as change, deadlines, and confrontations, are part of everyday life in the professional kitchen. These pressures cause 6. _____, a physical, mental, and emotional response to external pressures. Of course, there are many other foodservice professions to consider. They all require training. 7. _____ _____, for example, are nutrition professionals who have completed at minimum a bachelor's degree in dietetics, an internship, and passed a national exam.

Whatever you decide, good luck with your career plans!

Master Chef

What It Takes to Be a Chef

Chapter 4

Activity B

Name _____

Date _____Period_____

Part 1: The Roles Chefs Fulfill

To successfully run a commercial kitchen, a chef must fulfill many roles including *cook, leader, manager, artistic innovator, teacher,* and *mentor*. Complete the following statements with the appropriate role.

1. Chefs taking the role of _____ create new dishes for daily specials and market menus. Occasionally, they create an entirely new menu.

2. Chefs taking the role of _____ judge the quality of food products being prepared by the cooks.

3. Chefs taking the role of _____ manage both people and resources.

4. Chefs taking the role of _____ teach the staff cooking skills, management skills, how to deal with people, and more.

5. Chefs taking the role of _____ organize and direct the efforts of the kitchen staff to achieve their version of cuisine.

Part 2: Professional Traits of Successful Culinarians

Professionals are expected to demonstrate the following traits: *respectful, punctual and dependable, positive attitude, flexible, productivity and speed*. For each of the following examples of culinary professional behavior, write the trait being demonstrated.

_____ 6. Works efficiently.

_____ 7. Regularly comes to work on time.

_____ 8. Not easily discouraged.

_____ 9. Responds to unexpected events and adjusts plans as needed.

_____ 10. Treats people of all cultures with equal courtesy.

_____ 11. Adapts cooking methods or menu to fluctuations in resources.

_____ 12. Balances speed, accuracy, and safety.

Reviewing Key Concepts

Chapter 4

Activity C

Name _____

Date _____ Period _____

Part 1: Knowledge and Expertise Chefs Must Have

In addition to being an expert cook, a chef must have expertise in several other areas. Match the area of expertise to the example of specific knowledge to which it best relates.

Examples of Specific Knowledge

_____ 1. The rules and procedures of table service.

_____ 2. How to interact well with diners and the public at large.

_____ 3. Basic mathematics and common bookkeeping procedures.

_____ 4. The latest information on nutrition.

_____ 5. How to manage preventive maintenance on appliances.

_____ 6. Microbiology and basic chemistry of sanitation management.

_____ 7. How to select, receive, and store the food used in the kitchen.

_____ 8. The laws that affect the foodservice industry.

_____ 9. How foods react chemically and physically during the cooking process.

Areas of Expertise

A. cost accounting

B. equipment maintenance

C. food and beverage service

D. food chemistry and physics

E. laws of the foodservice industry

F. nutrition

G. public relations

H. purchasing and storekeeping

I. sanitation

(Continued)

Activity C *(Continued)*   **Name** _____

Part 2: Education and Training in the Culinary Arts

Match the following terms and identifying phrases.

_____ 10. Is learning and achievement by work experience.

_____ 11. Are evidence of the evolution of chefs to be regarded as professionals rather than tradespeople.

_____ 12. Have begun to offer culinary and hospitality training and made the courses career focused.

_____ 13. Are ways to learn a trade under the guidance of skilled tradespeople.

_____ 14. Is considered by many to be the standard level of education for culinary management positions.

_____ 15. Is considered essential for all culinary professionals because of the dynamic conditions of the field.

_____ 16. Internships and work-based experience are part of the programs offered here.

A. apprenticeships

B. associate's degree

C. bachelor's and advanced degrees in culinary arts

D. career tech and technical high schools

E. high schools

F. lifelong learning

G. on-the-job training

Part 3: Allied Professions

In addition to a career as a chef, Chapter 4 discusses many other professional options in foodservice. These professions require knowledge and skills similar to those of a chef. Next to each of the following statements, write one of the professions discussed in Chapter 4 that best matches the stated preference or interest.

_____ 17. Likes to write about food.

_____ 18. Has the ability to teach.

_____ 19. Wants to help increase the public's food knowledge and culinary skill to improve nutrition and health status.

_____ 20. Interested in selling and promoting.

_____ 21. Interested in working in a manufacturing plant rather than a restaurant kitchen.

_____ 22. Wants to cook for just one family.

_____ 23. Wants to advise other professionals.

Sanitation Hazards

Culinary Terminology

Chapter 5

Activity A

Name _____

Date _____ Period _____

Part 1

Match the following terms and identifying phrases.

_____ 1. The measure of acidity or alkalinity of a substance.

_____ 2. Consists of harmful organisms that cause foodborne illness.

_____ 3. The amount of water available for microbial growth in a product.

_____ 4. Bacteria that requires oxygen.

_____ 5. Any illness caused by eating contaminated food.

_____ 6. The creation and practice of clean and healthy food-handling habits.

_____ 7. The unwanted presence of harmful substances or levels of dangerous microorganisms in food.

_____ 8. Bacteria that thrive without oxygen.

_____ 9. An organism that lives in and feeds on the body of another live creature.

_____ 10. A microscopic fungus that consumes sugar and expels alcohol and carbon dioxide gas.

_____ 11. Occurs when the body interprets a normally harmless protein as a dangerous substance.

_____ 12. Single-celled organisms that reproduce by dividing.

A. aerobic bacteria

B. allergy

C. anaerobic bacteria

D. bacteria

E. biological hazard

F. contamination

G. foodborne illness

H. parasite

I. pH

J. sanitation

K. water activity

L. yeast

(Continued)

Activity A *(Continued)*   Name _____

Part 2

_____ 13. List the composition of a chemical product, proper procedures for storage and handling, and what to do in case of an emergency.

_____ 14. Foods that support bacterial growth.

_____ 15. Illness resulting from ingestion of bacteria that create or contain toxins, or poisonous substances, that are harmful to humans.

_____ 16. Temperature range [41°F–135°F (5°C–57.2°C)] in which bacteria reproduce rapidly.

_____ 17. Any chemical that contaminates food.

_____ 18. A very small organism that invades another cell and causes it to reproduce the virus.

_____ 19. Solid materials that pose a danger to the consumer when present in food.

_____ 20. A thick-walled, "supersurvival unit."

_____ 21. Bacteria that can grow either with or without oxygen.

_____ 22. Illness resulting from live bacteria.

_____ 23. An organism that is dangerous to humans.

_____ 24. The name for a large family of single-cell fungi.

A. chemical hazard

B. facultative bacteria

C. infection

D. intoxication

E. material safety data sheets (MSDS)

F. mold

G. pathogen

H. physical hazard

I. potentially hazardous food

J. spore

K. temperature danger zone

L. virus

Identifying Hazards

Chapter 5   Name _____

Activity B   Date _____ Period _____

1. Select the appropriate food terms or procedures from the following list to complete the "Bacteria" chart below. Place the letter from each correct selection in the appropriate box. (Some terms and procedures will not be used.)

   A. Limit time in temperature danger zone   G. Add water to food

   B. Dried fruits   H. Remove water from food

   C. High protein foods   I. Cut tomatoes

   D. Add alkaline ingredients to food   J. Handle high protein and other
                                                        potentially hazardous foods with care
   E. Reduce amount of oxygen available to
      bacteria   K. Add acidic ingredients to food

   F. Raw seed sprouts   L. Store food between 41°F and 135°F

Bacteria	
Favored food sources	
Ways to control growth	

2. Repeat the steps described above to complete the "Viruses" chart below.

   A. Buy food in bulk   F. Raw or undercooked shellfish

   B. Buy food only from reputable suppliers   G. Wash raw vegetables before eating

   C. Raw salad ingredients   H. Practice excellent personal hygiene

   D. Hard cooked eggs   I. Add acidic ingredients to food

   E. Expose food to open air   J. Avoid shellfish from polluted waters

Viruses	
Likely food sources	
Ways to avoid contamination	

(Continued)

Activity B *(Continued)*   **Name** _____

3. Review the information in Chapter 5 and complete the remaining charts.

Fungi			
Types that cause food contamination			
Characteristics			

Parasites		
Type of Parasite	**Common Food Source(s)**	**How to Prevent Transmission**
Trichinella spiralis		
Anisakis, **and certain varieties of** *cestodes* **and** *trematodes*		

Fish Toxins		
Toxin		
Fish commonly associated with toxin		

Reviewing Key Concepts

Chapter 5

Activity C

Name _____

Date _____ Period _____

Part 1: Working with Food Safely

Read each statement below. Circle the letter *T* if the statement is true. If the statement is false, circle *F* and write the corrected statement on the lines that follow.

T   F   1.   Improper food handling can result in foodborne illness.

_____

_____

T   F   2.   Foodborne illness is inconvenient but never serious.

_____

_____

T   F   3.   Outbreaks of foodborne illness can result in employees being fired.

_____

_____

T   F   4.   Businesses are not at risk of being sued by customers who contract foodborne illness.

_____

_____

T   F   5.   Serving food that is free of contamination is a goal and responsibility for management alone.

_____

_____

(Continued)

Activity C *(Continued)*   **Name** _____

Part 2: Classifying Food Safety Hazards

Food contamination can result from biological, chemical, or physical hazards. Classify the following contaminants by checking (✓) the correct column for each.

Contaminant	Types of Food Safety Hazards		
	Biological	**Chemical**	**Physical**
Bacteria			
Bleach			
Cleaning supplies			
Fish toxins			
Fungi			
Galvanized steel cookware			
Glass			
Herbicides			
Insecticides			
Metal shards			
Mold			
Parasites			
Pesticides			
Polishes			
Staples			
Toothpicks			
Viruses			
Zinc			

(Continued)

Activity C *(Continued)*   **Name** _____

Part 3: Preventing Chemical and Physical Hazards

Use terms from the following list to fill in the missing blanks in the statements below.

chemicals	metal	separate from
chewed	mix	spices
clearly marked	MSDS	staples
close to	original	supervisor
high	react	thrown out
manufacturer's	seen	

6. Store chemicals in_____ _____ containers or leave them in their _____ package.

7. Do not store food in containers that previously held _____.

8. Only use chemicals according to the _____ instructions.

9. Store chemicals in an area _____ _____ food preparation areas.

10. Never randomly _____ chemicals because certain chemicals can _____ to create highly poisonous substances.

11. If uncertain about how to use a chemical product, ask a _____.

12. Display _____ sheets in a visible and accessible place in the kitchen.

13. Do not store glass in _____ places. All food that might possibly be contaminated with glass should be _____ _____.

14. When breaking down boxes, be careful that _____ do not enter food.

15. Check contents of cans opened by commercial can openers for _____ shards.

16. When using toothpicks, be sure to use ones that are easily _____.

Notes

Sanitation Procedures

Culinary Terminology

Chapter 6

Activity A

Name _____

Date _____ Period _____

Complete the following statements about sanitation procedures. Then arrange the circled letters to solve problem 9.

1. Any surface such as a table, cutting board, or piece of equipment that comes in contact with food is considered a _ _ _O-_ _ _O_ _ _ _O_ _ _ _ _.

2. A _ _ _O_ _ _ _ environment is free from pathogens.

3. A_O_ _ _ _ _ _ _ _ _ _ _ _ _O_ _ _ _ _ is a licensed professional who uses various chemicals, sprays, and traps to prevent or eliminate infestations.

4. A step in food handling at which control can be applied to prevent or eliminate a food safety hazard is a _ _ _ _ _ _O_ _ _ _ _O_ _ _ _ _ _ _ _.

5. _O_ _ _-_ _ _O_ O_ _ _ _ _ _ _ _ occurs when harmful microorganisms are transferred from one product to another by hands, utensils, equipment, or other physical contact.

6. A_ _ _ _ _O_ _ _ _O_ _ _O_ _ _ _ _ _ _ consists of three adjacent sinks used to clean, rinse, and sanitize small equipment and utensils.

7. _ _ _O_ _ _ _ _ _ _ _ _ _ _ _ _ _O_ _ _ _ _ _ _ _ _ _ _ _ _ _ _ _ is a system that identifies and manages key steps in food handling where contamination is most likely to occur.

8. _ _O_O is the visual appearance that something is unsoiled.

Circled letters: _____

9. A key principle to food safety is _.

Reviewing Key Concepts

Chapter 6

Activity B

Name _____

Date _____ Period _____

Part 1: Time and Temperature

Circle the clue in parentheses that best completes each of the following statements.

1. To protect food from contamination, you must make sure food is (**above**) (**below**) (**above or below**) the temperature danger zone.

2. When food must be in the temperature danger zone, limit the time to no more than (**twelve**) (**eight**) (**four**) (**two**) hours.

3. Thaw frozen food in the refrigerator or under (**hot**) (**warm**) (**cold**) running water.

4. To kill biological hazards present in most foods, cook to an (**internal**) (**external**) (**approximate**) temperature of 145°F (62.8°C).

5. Food held hot must maintain an (**internal**) (**external**) (**approximate**) temperature of (**145°F [62.8°C]**) (**135°F [57.2°C]**) or more.

6. Hot, fully cooked food must be cooled (**slowly**) (**quickly**).

Part 2: Cross-Contamination

Read the following scenarios. In the space provided, explain where the cross-contamination could occur and how it could be avoided.

7. A cook is assembling cold sandwich plates for a luncheon. A coworker invites him to sign a "get well" card for a sick employee. The cook stops what he is doing, borrows the pen from the coworker, and signs the card. The cook returns to preparing his plates. ____

    _____

    _____

    _____

8. A cook cleans and sanitizes her work counter before beginning her assignment. A coworker comes by and asks to borrow a knife. The cook grabs her toolbox and places it on the counter. She finds the knife in her tool box and loans it to her coworker. She returns her toolbox to its storage place and proceeds with food preparation on her work counter. _____

    _____

    _____

    _____

(Continued)

Activity B *(Continued)*   Name _____

9. A cook seasons some raw chicken breasts and lays them out on a sheet pan. He stores the chicken in the refrigerator until he is ready to cook them. The cook places the pan of chicken on the top shelf in the refrigerator because the shelves below are filled with dessert parfaits for a luncheon. _____

_____

_____

_____

Part 3: Cleaning and Sanitizing

10. Explain the following statement: "A kitchen can look clean and still be unsanitary." _____

_____

_____

_____

For each of the following cleaning and sanitizing techniques, indicate the order in which these steps must be performed. In the space provided, assign each step a number to indicate its order in the sequence. The first step is assigned the number "1" and so on.

Technique for Sanitizing a Counter or Worktable	
Sequence of Steps	**Steps**
	Rinse table using hot water and a clean towel.
	Wash the table with hot water and detergent.
	Allow to air-dry.
	Clear table or countertop.
	Apply sanitizer using either a spray bottle or a special sanitizing bucket.

Technique for Using a Dishmachine	
Sequence of Steps	**Steps**
	Remove visible pieces of food before placing items into machine.
	Load the rack into the dishmachine.
	Presoak flatware to loosen encrusted food.
	When the cleaning and sanitizing cycles are complete, allow items to air-dry.
	Place the items to be washed in the appropriate dish rack.

(Continued)

Activity B *(Continued)*   **Name** _____

Technique for Cleaning and Sanitizing Large Equipment	
Sequence of Steps	**Steps**
	Sanitize using a sanitizing solution.
	Dry using a clean towel or paper towels.
	Unplug equipment.
	Disassemble equipment as needed.
	Put on cut-resistant gloves if washing a sharp piece of machinery.
	Rinse with hot water.
	Wash with hot water and detergent to remove visible grime and food.

Reviewing Key Concepts

Chapter 6

Activity C

Name _____

Date _____ **Period** _____

Part 1: Personal Hygiene

Select the term or phrase from the following list that best completes each statement below. (Some terms will be used more than once.)

20	communal	roll up sleeves
40	elbows	six
air dryer	every	sweat
antimicrobial	four	under
backs	gloved	warm
change	hot	
comfortable	paper towel	

A. Technique for proper hand washing

1. Use water that is as hot as is _____.

2. _____ and wet your hands.

3. Add _____ soap and lather hands, including the _____ and wrists, and up to the _____. Scrub for _____ seconds and use a nailbrush to scrub _____ the fingernails. Wash well between fingers.

4. Rinse under _____, running water.

5. Dry using _____ or _____. Do not dry hands on a _____ towel or apron.

6. Use _____ to turn water off and open bathroom door, then discard.

B. Guidelines for using disposable gloves

7. Properly wash hands using _____ soap before putting on a pair of gloves.

8. Change gloves if _____ starts to drip from under gloves.

9. Change gloves after_____ work task.

10. If gloves become even slightly torn or punctured, _____ them.

11. Change gloves at least every _____ hours.

12. Never wash _____ hands.

(Continued)

Activity C *(Continued)*   **Name** _____

Part 2: Insect, Rodent, and Waste Control

Answer the following questions in the space provided.

13. Name two ways that insects and rodents spread biological hazards in the kitchen. (Relate to pest droppings and garbage.) _____

_____

_____

_____

14. What is the most important step in pest control?_____

_____

15. What is the minimum frequency for emptying garbage containers in the kitchen?_____

_____

Part 3: Hazard Analysis Critical Control Point and Health Inspection

Complete the following statements in the space provided.

16. The goal of the Hazard Analysis Critical Control Point (HACCP) system is to _____

_____

_____

_____ .

17. HACCP pays particular attention to the temperature danger zone and _____

_____ .

18. HACCP plans rely on predetermined critical control points (CCP). CCP is a step in food handling at which control can be applied to _____ or _____ a food safety hazard.

19. Health inspectors are responsible for protecting the _____ health.

20. When a health department official inspects a foodservice operation, foodservice workers should answer their questions _____ .

Safety in the Kitchen

Culinary Terminology

Chapter 7

Activity A

Name _____

Date _____ Period _____

Under each of the culinary terms that follow is a list of statements. If the statement is accurate, place a check (✓) in the space provided before each statement.

Fire Extinguisher

_____ 1. Commercial kitchens are required by law to have them.

_____ 2. Are all the same.

_____ 3. Are pressurized canisters filled with a substance that puts fires out.

Heat Exhaustion

_____ 4. Is more serious than heatstroke.

_____ 5. Is a heat-related condition that results when the body loses too much water and salt.

_____ 6. Is often brought on by heatstroke.

_____ 7. Can be brought on by working at a fast pace in a hot environment.

Heatstroke

_____ 8. Is more serious than heat exhaustion.

_____ 9. Is a condition in which the body's usual ability to deal with heat stress is lost.

_____ 10. Is potentially life threatening and requires immediate medical attention.

_____ 11. Can be brought on by heat exhaustion.

Kitchen Hood Fire Suppression System

_____ 12. Required by law for commercial kitchens.

_____ 13. Is an installed, comprehensive fire fighting system that automatically sounds an alarm when a fire is detected.

_____ 14. Is an installed, comprehensive fire fighting system that automatically puts out a fire before it spreads.

Occupational Safety and Health Administration

_____ 15. Is commonly known as OSHA.

_____ 16. Requires all workplaces to post the Occupational Safety and Health Administration's safety and health poster and a yearly log of injury and illness.

_____ 17. Is a government agency that defines and enforces safe working conditions.

Roles in Creating Workplace Safety

Chapter 7   Name _____

Activity B   Date _____ Period_____

Government, employers, and employees all play a part in creating a safe workplace. Circle the group (or groups) to whom the workplace safety rights and responsibilities listed in the left column applies.

Workplace Safety Rights and Responsibilities	Who Is Responsible? (Circle all that apply)		
Must maintain a safe workplace by law.	government	employers	employees
Must keep accident reports on file permanently for future reference.	government	employers	employees
Ensures that employers train their employees in safe work practices.	government	employers	employees
Can contact OSHA for advice and help.	government	employers	employees
Along with witnesses, are asked to fill out accident report forms when accidents occur.	government	employers	employees
Are held responsible for all safety information presented during safety training.	government	employers	employees

Dress for Safety

Chapter 7

Activity C

Name _____

Date _____ **Period** _____

Complete the following statements that describe the safety features of the professional culinary uniform.

The Chef Jacket...

1. ...is white *because* _____

_____

_____ .

2. ...is long sleeved *because* _____

_____

_____ .

3. ...is double-breasted *because* _____

_____

_____ .

The Chef Pants...

4. ...are long *because* _____

_____

_____ .

The Apron...

5. ...is not to be used for wiping hands *because* _____

_____

_____ .

6. ...is designed to be easily lifted from the body *because* _____

_____

_____ .

(Continued)

Activity C *(Continued)*   **Name** _____

Footwear...

7. ...ideally has nonslip soles *because* _____

_____

_____.

8. ...is never open-toed *because* _____

_____

_____.

Jewelry

9. Rings, necklaces, earrings, and bracelets should not be worn in the kitchen *because* _____

_____

_____

_____.

10. Small pieces of jewelry, such as used in piercings, should not be worn in the kitchen *because* __

_____

_____

_____.

Kitchen Injuries

Chapter 7   **Name** _____

Activity D   **Date** _____ **Period** _____

Select the term or phrase from the following list that best completes the statements about kitchen injuries below. Some terms or phrases will not be used.

announce	dishwashing	leather
appropriate	downward	nonslip
away	dull	promptly
catch	eventually	read
chop	gesture	rubber mats
clear	greasy	run or push
cotton rugs	holding	sharp
cutting	kitchen	upward

A. Preventing cuts

1. Practice correct knife_____ skills.

2. Always carry a knife by your side and pointed _____ .

3. Always _____ when you are carrying a knife to warn others of the danger.

4. Never leave a knife or sharp object in a_____ sink.

5. Never_____ with a knife.

6. Never try to _____ a falling knife.

7. Use only _____ knives.

8. Use knives only for _____tasks, never as hammers or can openers.

B. Preventing falls

9. Make sure spills are _____ wiped up.

10. Clean _____floors immediately.

11. No matter how busy you are, do not _____ in the kitchen.

12. Place removable _____ wherever the floor is slippery.

13. Keep aisles _____ .

14. Wear shoes with _____ soles.

15. Put ladders and stools _____ after using them.

Fire Safety

Chapter 7

Activity E

Name _____

Date _____Period_____

Part 1: Ingredients for Fire

Three ingredients must always be present to produce fire—*fuel, oxygen,* and *heat*. Indicate which of these ingredient(s) is being removed from each of the scenarios below.

1. The chef would not allow newspapers to be left lying around in the kitchen. Which ingredient for fire did the chef want to remove? _____

2. When a sauté pan caught fire, the cook grabbed a cover and placed it on the pan. Which ingredient for fire did the cook want to remove? _____

3. The chef insisted that spilled grease be wiped off the stove immediately. Which ingredient for fire did the cook want to remove? _____

4. The server extinguished the candle by blowing on it. Which ingredient for fire did the server want to remove? _____

5. The culinary worker threw water on a potholder that caught fire. Which ingredients for fire did the cook want to remove? _____ and _____

Part 2: Using Fire Extinguishers

Circle the clue in parentheses that best completes each of the following statements.

6. Use a fire extinguisher only if the fire is (**spreading rapidly**) (**localized**).

7. Position yourself with your (**back**) (**face**) toward an exit.

8. (**Take time**) (**Don't take time**) to verify that you have the correct extinguisher for the type of fire.

9. Pull the pin at the (**top**) (**nozzle**) of the fire extinguisher.

10. Aim at the (**top**) (**base**) of the flames.

11. (**Squeeze**) (**Grip**) the trigger.

12. Sweep (**up and down**) (**back and forth**) so the entire base of the fire is covered repeatedly.

13. Continue to spray until the fire is (**diminished**) (**out**).

Knives and Hand Tools in the Professional Kitchen

Culinary Terminology

Name _____

Date _____ Period _____

Match the following terms and identifying phrases.

_____ 1. A rod used to keep the blade sharp as you work.

_____ 2. Called a melon baller by home cooks.

_____ 3. A type of steel used to make knives that sharpens well but rusts easily. It also loses its shine and discolors quickly after its first use.

_____ 4. The portion of the knife blade that extends into the handle of the knife.

_____ 5. A type of steel used to make knives that is difficult to sharpen, but does not pit, rust, or discolor; and does not affect the flavor of foods.

_____ 6. Long-handled tool used to strain items or lift them out of liquid.

_____ 7. The thick metal collar on some knives that runs from the heel of the blade to the handle.

_____ 8. A flat, abrasive stone used to sharpen a knife once its edge is dull and worn.

_____ 9. A type of metal used to make most good quality professional knives.

A. bolster

B. carbon steel

C. high-carbon stainless steel

D. Parisienne scoop

E. spider

F. stainless steel

G. steel

H. tang

I. whetstone

The Art and Science of Knife Construction

Chapter 8

Activity B

Name _____

Date _____ Period _____

Three types of metal—carbon steel, stainless steel, and high-carbon stainless steel—are used for knife blades. In the chart below, circle the metal(s) that best fits the description in the column on the left. Some answers include more than one metal.

Description of Metal	Type of Metal (circle all that apply)		
Does not rust or discolor.	carbon steel	stainless steel	high-carbon stainless steel
Easiest to sharpen to a finely honed edge.	carbon steel	stainless steel	high-carbon stainless steel
Loses its shine and discolors quickly after its first use.	carbon steel	stainless steel	high-carbon stainless steel
Metal of which most good quality professional knives are made.	carbon steel	stainless steel	high-carbon stainless steel
Can transfer a metallic flavor to foods.	carbon steel	stainless steel	high-carbon stainless steel
Is so hard, it is difficult to sharpen and keep sharp.	carbon steel	stainless steel	high-carbon stainless steel
Will rust if left in a damp place.	carbon steel	stainless steel	high-carbon stainless steel

Answer the following questions about knife construction.

1. What is a full tang? _____

_____

2. Why is a knife with a full tang better than one with a rattail tang? _____

_____

3. What is the specific purpose of a bolster? _____

_____

4. What is a balanced knife? _____

_____

Reviewing Key Concepts

Chapter 8

Activity C

Name _____

Date _____Period_____

Part 1: Using a Steel and Whetstone

Circle the clue in parentheses that best completes each of the following statements.

1. The steel **(is a rod used to keep the blade sharp as you work)** **(is a flat, abrasive stone used to sharpen a knife once its edge is dull and worn)**.

2. When using a steel, use **(slight)** **(moderate)** **(full)** force when stroking the steel and keep the edge of the knife at a **(20)** **(45)** **(60)**-degree angle to the steel.

3. There are two methods for using a steel. In one method, you hold the steel in front of you and **(parallel)** **(perpendicular)** to your body. For the other method, place the tip of the steel on the cutting board and hold it so the steel is **(horizontal)** **(vertical)**.

4. Both methods for using a steel require that the blade be honed **(only where worn)** **(the full length of the blade)**.

5. The whetstone **(is a rod used to keep the blade sharp as you work)** **(is a flat, abrasive stone used to sharpen a knife once its edge is dull and worn)**.

6. Most chefs lubricate the whetstone to make sharpening easier. Two lubricants typically used for sharpening in the professional kitchen are **(vegetable oil and butter)** **(olive oil and water)** **(mineral oil and water)**.

7. When sharpening, begin with the **(fine)** **(coarse)** side of the stone.

8. When using the whetstone, hold the knife at a **(20)** **(45)** **(60)**-degree angle to the surface of the stone.

9. Begin with the heel of the blade in the **(lower right)** **(upper left)** corner of the stone. Repeat the process on the other side of the blade. Begin with the heel in the **(lower left)** **(upper right)** corner of the stone.

10. After using the stone, finish the edge by honing it on **(the fine side of the whetstone)** **(the coarse side of the whetstone)** **(the steel)**.

Activity C   **Name** _____

Part 2: Knives in the Professional Kitchen

Match the following terms and identifying phrases.

_____ 11. Has a long, narrow, flexible blade. Using a light sawing motion allows you to cut cooked meat and poultry into thin, even slices.

_____ 12. Has an inwardly curved blade that makes the job of cutting vegetables into small football shapes easier.

_____ 13. Is easily identified by its large rectangular blade, which is used for chopping.

_____ 14. Have flexible blades, but are not sharp. Used for spreading coatings on food or as a spatula to turn food while cooking.

_____ 15. A smaller version of the chef knife, typically with a blade between 5 and 7 inches long.

_____ 16. Is the most used knife in any chef's knife kit and sometimes called a *French knife*. Has various length blades.

_____ 17. Blade is about 6 inches long. Used for separating muscle from bone on meat or poultry, or for filleting and portioning fish.

_____ 18. Not sharp, but has a pointed end, which is used to pry apart shells of oysters.

_____ 19. Small, short-bladed knife designed to cut away skin or peel.

_____ 20. Short knife with a 1-inch wide blade that tapers to an edge, but is not sharp. Used for opening clams, not for cutting.

_____ 21. Also called a *butcher's knife*. Has a long, thick, highly curved blade.

_____ 22. Has teeth like a saw and is used for cutting breads and pastries.

A. boning and filet knives

B. chef knife

C. clam knife

D. cleaver

E. oyster knife

F. palette knives and spreaders

G. paring knife

H. scimitar

I. serrated slice

J. slicer

K. tourné knife

L. utility knife

Activity C   **Name** _____

Part 3: Hand Tools in the Professional Kitchen

Answer the following questions in the space provided.

23. Why have wooden cutting boards recently returned to commercial kitchens?_____

_____

_____

_____

24. For what type of task is the Parisienne scoop designed? _____

_____

_____

25. For what type of task can both a skimmer and a spider be used?_____

_____

_____

Knife Skills

Culinary Terminology

Name _____

Date _____ Period _____

Match the following terms and identifying phrases.

_____ 1. A round slice cut from round food such as carrots. It is often ¼-inch (6 mm) thick.

_____ 2. Portion of food cut into stick shapes that are 2 x ¼ x ¼ inch (50 x 6 x 6 mm).

_____ 3. Portion of food cut into stick shapes that are 2 x ⅛ x ⅛ inch (50 x 3 x 3 mm).

_____ 4. Portion of food cut first into sticks and then into cubes ¾ x ¾ x ¾ inch (2 x 2 x 2 cm).

_____ 5. Portion of food cut first into sticks and then into cubes ½ x ½ x ½ inch (13 x 13 x 13 mm).

_____ 6. Portion of food cut first into sticks and then into cubes ¼ x ¼ x ¼ inch (6 x 6 x 6 mm).

_____ 7. Portion of food cut first into sticks and then into cubes ⅛ x ⅛ x ⅛ inch (3 x 3 x 3 mm).

_____ 8. Portion of food cut first into sticks and then into rectangles ½ x ½ x ¼ inch (13 x 13 x 6 mm).

_____ 9. The process of chopping food into very fine pieces.

_____ 10. A seven-sided football shape. Vegetables are often cut into this shape in high-end restaurants.

A. batonnet

B. brunoise

C. julienne

D. large dice

E. medium dice

F. mincing

G. paysanne

H. rondelle

I. small dice

J. tourné

Numerical Patterns in Knife Cuts

Chapter 9   **Name** _____

Activity B   **Date** _____ **Period** _____

Recognizing simple patterns in a numerical sequence or set of sequences can help you predict the next number or sequence. Some of the series of cuts used in the professional kitchen to prepare vegetables are examples of such sequences. Once you know the pattern, you can easily calculate the others.

One way to discover relationships in numerical sequences is to look for a pattern in the way each term relates to the one before it. For example, in the number sequence 0, 5, 10, 15, 20..., the pattern is that each term is 5 more than the one before it. It is reasonable to predict that the next number in the sequence would be 25.

A. Analyzing stick cut patterns

Analyze the patterns in the following two stick cuts, then answer the questions that follow.

Julienne: 2 x ⅛ x ⅛ inch

Batonnet: 2 x ¼ x ¼ inch

1. What stays the same in both cuts? _____
   What changes? _____

2. What is the numerical difference between the size of the sides in the julienne
   and the batonnet? _____

3. What is the pattern? _____

   _____

4. Some chefs use a smaller variation of julienne that is 2 x ¹⁄₁₆ x ¹⁄₁₆ inch. If you add this cut
   to the sequence, does the pattern change? _____

(Continued)

Activity B *(Continued)*   **Name** _____

B. Analyzing dice cut patterns

Analyze the numerical pattern of the following dice cuts, then answer the questions that follow.

Brunoise: ⅛ x ⅛ x ⅛ inch

Small dice: ¼ x ¼ x ¼ inch

Medium dice: ½ x ½ x ½ inch

5. What is the pattern of the size of the dice cuts? _____

   _____

6. The dimensions of large dice are ¾ x ¾ x ¾ inch. Does the large dice cut fit into the
   established pattern? Explain._____

   _____

   _____

   _____

7. What pattern can you describe to help you remember the dimensions of dice cuts? _____

   _____

   _____

   _____

   _____

   _____

Reviewing Key Concepts

Chapter 9

Activity C

Name _____

Date _____ Period _____

Part 1: Preparing a Cutting Workstation

Circle the clue in parentheses that best completes each of the following statements.

1. Select a (**cleaned and dried**) (**cleaned and sanitized**) cutting board.

2. Place a (**damp**) (**dry**) towel between the cutting board and the (**vegetables**) (**worktable**).

3. Assess the height of the worktable and cutting board. If cutting board is too low, you can use a series of (**sheet trays**) (**towels**) to elevate it.

4. Select the appropriate knife and make sure the edge is (**sharp**) (**not too sharp**).

5. Stand facing the worktable. Feet should be (**shoulder-width apart**) (**close together**).

Part 2: Technique for Cutting with the Chef Knife

Read each statement below. Circle the letter *T* if the statement is true. If the statement is false, circle *F* and write the corrected statement on the lines that follow.

T   F   6. Position the guiding hand on one or several smaller objects. Be sure the thumb and pinky are holding the objects securely and are behind the other fingers. The front fingers are curved.

_____

_____

T   F   7. Place the flat side of the knife against the end joint of the front fingers of the guiding hand.

_____

_____

T   F   8. Gently glide the chef knife in the proper forward and backward motion until the tip of the blade is resting on the cutting board.

_____

_____

T   F   9. Lift the back end of the knife so that the tip remains pointing down. Slide the guiding hand back to the location of the next cut.

_____

_____

(Continued)

Activity C *(Continued)*   Name _____

Part 3: Technique for Using the Boning Knife, Paring Knife, Slicer, and Serrated Bread Knife

Answer the following questions in the space provided.

10. Which of the following is *not* a correct technique for gripping a boning knife. _____

    A. All the fingers grip the handle of the knife as if shaking someone's hand.

    B. The thumb and forefinger grasp the portion of the knife blade just next to the end of the handle.

    C. All the fingers except the index finger grip the handle. The index finger rests on the back of the blade.

    D. All the fingers wrap around the handle with the blade pointing down.

11. When using the chef's knife, the guiding hand directly guides the knife during cutting. When using a boning knife, what does the guiding hand do?_____

    _____

12. When making a tourné with a paring knife, do you draw the knife from top to bottom or bottom to top? _____

13. Which is correct when making a tourné, making a series of even short cuts or one long continuous cut? _____

14. After the first cut on the tourné, how much do you turn the vegetable before making the next cut? _____

15. How many equal sides should a finished tourné have? _____

16. The slicer and serrated bread knife are used in similar manners. The hand is wrapped around the handle like a handshake. How many fingers are kept on the blade? _____

    _____

17. When using a slicer or serrated bread knife, should the knife stroke be a long and sawing motion or short with strong downward pressure? _____

    _____

18. When using a slicer or serrated bread knife, should the knife hand be held tight or relaxed during slicing?_____

Notes

Smallwares

Culinary Terminology

Chapter 10

Activity A

Name _____

Date _____ Period_____

Circle the clue in parentheses that best completes each of the following statements.

1. A (**mandoline**) (**rondeau**) (**chinois**) is a wide pan with 6 to 8 inch (15 to 21 cm) sides and two looped handles.

2. A large bowl-shaped strainer used to drain large quantities of product is a (**mandoline**) (**rondeau**) (**colander**).

3. Sautoir is a sauté pan (**with sloped or rounded sides**) (**with straight sides**) (**also called a Griswold**).

4. Sauteuse is a sauté pan (**with sloped or rounded sides**) (**with straight sides**) (**also called a Griswold**).

5. A cone-shaped strainer used to remove lumps and particles from liquids such as sauces is a (**mandoline**) (**china cap**) (**rondeau**).

6. To cook foods gently in hot water, chefs use a (**china cap**) (**mandoline**) (**bain marie**).

7. Pots, pans, and other hand tools used to prepare food are called (**bain marie**) (**smallwares**) (**rondeau**).

8. (**Hotel pans**) (**Sheet pans**) (**Chinois**) are rectangular stainless steel pans used to hold food in steam tables, warmers, and refrigerators.

9. (**Hotel pans**) (**Sheet pans**) (**Chinois**) are larger, shallow pans used for baking and food storage.

10. A (**pot**) (**pan**) (**colander**) is a cooking container that is as tall, or taller, than it is wide.

11. A (**sautoir**) (**sauteuse**) (**chinois**) is a type of china cap that has a finely woven, metal mesh.

12. A (**pot**) (**pan**) (**chinois**) is a cooking container that is wider than it is tall.

13. To chop large quantities of food, chefs use a machine called a (**mandoline**) (**conduction**) (**buffalo chopper**).

14. A device used to slice food by pushing the food onto and across a shaper metal blade is a (**mandoline**) (**conduction**) (**buffalo chopper**).

15. (**Mandoline**) (**Conduction**) (**Bain marie**) is the term used to describe how well pots and pans transfer heat from the burner or oven to the food they contain.

Using a Scientific Approach to Evaluate Cookware

Chapter 10

Activity B

Name _____

Date _____Period_____

Use your textbook as a resource to complete the charts below. Circle the term that best describes each property for that material. If the information is not available in your text, circle *Unknown*. When you have completed the charts, answer the questions that follow.

Copper			
Property	**Circle one for each property**		
Conduction	excellent	good	poor	unknown
Reacts with food	yes	no		unknown
Tarnish resistant	yes	no		unknown
Weight	heavy	medium	light	unknown
Cost	high	moderate	low	unknown

Aluminum			
Property	**Circle one for each property**		
Conduction	excellent	good	poor	unknown
Reacts with food	yes	no		unknown
Tarnish resistant	yes	no		unknown
Weight	heavy	medium	light	unknown
Cost	high	medium	low	unknown

Stainless Steel			
Property	**Circle one for each property**		
Conduction	excellent	good	poor	unknown
Reacts with food	yes	no		unknown
Tarnish resistant	yes	no		unknown
Weight	heavy	medium	light	unknown
Cost	high	medium	low	unknown

(Continued)

Activity B *(Continued)*   **Name** _____

1. Aluminum is the most widely used material for commercial cookware. What factor(s) do you think contributes most to it being the preferred material? Explain your answer. _____

   _____

   _____

2. Copper pans are often lined with stainless steel. What would be the advantage of that combination? _____

   _____

   _____

3. The best stainless steel pans have copper bottoms. What would be the advantage of that combination? _____

   _____

   _____

   _____

Reviewing Key Concepts

Chapter 10   Name _____

Activity C   Date _____Period_____

Part 1: Measuring and Portioning Tasks

Circle the clue in parentheses that best completes each of the following statements.

1. Containers used for measuring volume come in several sizes. Their capacities range from one cup to several (**cups**) (**quarts**) (**gallons**).

2. Sets of measuring spoons are useful for measuring small amounts of ingredients such as (**sugar and salt**) (**herbs and spices**) (**sugar and spices**). Measuring spoons range in size from an eighth of a teaspoon up to (**one teaspoon**) (**one tablespoon**) (**two tablespoons**).

3. To measure large quantities of food when it is delivered to the kitchen, foodservice operations use a (**portion**) (**balance-beam**) (**receiving**) scale.

4. To measure small quantities and individual ingredients, foodservice operations use a (**portion**) (**balance-beam**) (**receiving**) scale.

5. A (**portion**) (**balance-beam**) (**receiving**) scale has two platforms and a set of counterweights.

6. Bakers and pastry chefs typically use a (**portion**) (**balance-beam**) (**receiving**) scale to measure large amounts of dry ingredients.

7. Some (**bimetallic coil**) (**laser**) (**thermocouple**) (**candy**) thermometers can be placed in an oven and the meter placed outside the oven so it can be easily monitored.

8. Another name for a deep-fat thermometer is the (**bimetallic coil**) (**laser**) (**thermocouple**) (**candy**) thermometer.

9. One disadvantage of the (**bimetallic coil**) (**laser**) (**thermocouple**) (**candy**) thermometer is that they only measure the temperature on the surface and not internally.

Part 2: Straining Equipment

Circle the clue in parentheses that best completes each of the following statements.

10. A (**china cap**) (**chinois**) is a type of (**china cap**) (**chinois**) that has a finely woven, metal mesh.

11. The sieve through which cooked foods, usually potatoes, are placed and forced through with the plunger is a (**drum sieve**) (**ricer**).

(Continued)

Activity C (*Continued*)   Name _____

Part 3: Cutting and Processing Equipment

Match the following terms and identifying phrases.

_____ 12. A hollow, metal box with different size teeth on each side. It's used for shredding vegetables, cheese, chocolate, citrus peel, and spices.

_____ 13. A device used to slice food by pushing the food onto and across a sharp metal blade.

_____ 14. A two-part machine consisting of a motorized base and a covered container. The food to be processed is placed in the container and a lid covers the top to prevent splash.

_____ 15. An auger forces the food through a feed tube, past a rotating blade, and through the holes of the die. Used to process meat or other foods into various textures.

_____ 16. A one-piece machine consisting of a motorized shaft with blades on the end. The shaft and the blades are immersed in a container of liquid to purée the product.

_____ 17. Consists of a rotating bowl into which the food is placed. The bowl then passes under a set of rotating blades that chop the food into small pieces.

_____ 18. Uses a rotating blade to slice foods thinly and evenly.

_____ 19. Used primarily to grind, purée, and blend, but has cutting attachments that can produce shredded, julienned, and diced foods in a wide range of sizes.

A. bar blender

B. buffalo chopper

C. food processors

D. grater

E. immersion blender

F. mandoline

G. meat grinder

H. slicer

Large Equipment 11

Culinary Terminology

Chapter 11

Activity A

Name _____

Date _____ Period _____

Match the following terms and identifying phrases.

_____ 1. The most common type of commercial cooktop. Pots or pans are placed on trivets directly over a gas flame burner.

_____ 2. A permanently fixed, large pot with double-walled construction. It is a quick and efficient way to heat large quantities of liquid because the interior is heated with pressurized steam.

_____ 3. A polished stainless steel cooktop on which food is cooked directly without pots or pans.

_____ 4. A list of tasks to be performed to ensure that equipment stays in proper working order.

_____ 5. A radiant heat source placed above the food to be cooked.

_____ 6. A device that responds to temperature changes and either turns the burner on or off.

_____ 7. Small broiler, less powerful than regular broilers, used for browning food rather than fully cooking it.

_____ 8. Oven with a fan that helps circulate the hot air inside the oven.

_____ 9. Range with a heavy cast-iron top that has a heat source located underneath the top. Pots and pans are placed on the top and heated by conduction.

_____ 10. Oven that uses both heat and steam to cook foods.

_____ 11. Cooking appliance that has the radiant heat source located below the food and rack.

_____ 12. A cooktop that uses electromagnetic energy to heat special pots and pans made of magnetic metals.

A. broiler

B. combination oven

C. convection oven

D. flattop range

E. griddle

F. grill

G. induction burner

H. open-burner range

I. preventive maintenance schedule

J. salamander

K. steam-jacketed kettle

L. thermostat

The Best Equipment for the Job

Chapter 11

Name _____

Activity B

Date _____ **Period** _____

Select the appliance from the list that is best suited for each function described below. Write your answer in the space provided. Some terms will not be used.

broiler	griddle	salamander
combination oven	grill	steam-jacketed kettle
convection oven	open-burner range	tilt braiser
convection steamer	pressure fryer	
flattop range	pressure steamer	

Function

Cooking Appliance Recommended

1. Heat food in medium-sized pots while maintaining instant control of the heat.   _____

2. Brown food rather than fully cook it.   _____

3. Quickly heat 80 gallons (303 L) of soup stock.   _____

4. Use several pots and pans at the same time; instant control of heat isn't necessary.   _____

5. Cook food on a rack with heat source located below.   _____

6. Braise large quantities of product.   _____

7. Steam food that could be easily ruined by overcooking.   _____

8. Roast food, which is very vulnerable to drying out, as quickly as possible.   _____

9. Cook eggs, sandwiches, and pancakes in a short-order establishment.   _____

10. Cook food on a rack with heat source located above.   _____

11. Bake foods at an even temperature.   _____

Reviewing Key Concepts

Chapter 11

Activity C

Name _____

Date _____ Period _____

Part 1: Holding Equipment

Two common pieces of holding equipment are steam tables and warming cabinets. Place a check (✓) under the piece of equipment described in each statement.

Holding Equipment		
Description	Steam Table	Warming Cabinet
Is sometimes referred to by the French term *bain marie*.		
May have features that maintain moisture in the cabinet.		
Is heated by an electric element.		
Holds hot food in hotel pans and metal inserts by surrounding them with hot water and steam.		
May be heated by gas or electric.		
Are placed in the area of the kitchen where food is plated for service.		

Part 2: Fryers

Circle the clue in parentheses that best completes each of the following statements.

1. Deep fryers cook food by (**coating**) (**submerging**) (**basting**) them in hot fat.

2. Fryers are found in (**only fast-food**) (**only fine-dining**) (**most**) restaurants.

3. A fry kettle with a tightly sealed lid is called a (**deep fryer**) (**pressure fryer**) (**steam-jacketed kettle**).

4. Deep fryers are classified by the amount of (**chicken**) (**donuts**) (**fat**) they hold.

5. In a pressure fryer, the pressurized kettle fries food (**rapidly**) (**slowly**).

(Continued)

Activity C *(Continued)*   **Name** _____

Part 3: Refrigeration

Identify the correct statement in each set of statements below. Place a check (✓) in the space before each correct statement.

6. _____ A. Refrigeration stores foods below 41°F (4°C).
   _____ B. Refrigeration stores foods at 0°F (-18°C).
   _____ C. Refrigeration stores foods above 32°F (0°C).

7. _____ A. Refrigerators are defined by their temperature range.
   _____ B. Refrigerators are defined by their size.
   _____ C. Refrigerators are defined by their shape.

8. _____ A. Freezers store foods below 41° F (4°C).
   _____ B. Freezers store foods at 0°F (-18°C).
   _____ C. Freezers store foods below 32°F (0°C).

9. _____ A. Refrigeration works by removing heat from the refrigerator compartment.
   _____ B. Refrigeration works by channeling cold air into the refrigerator compartment.

10. _____ A. Refrigeration equipment is typically located in one area in a commercial kitchen.
    _____ B. Refrigeration equipment is typically located throughout a commercial kitchen.

Part 4: Equipment Maintenance

Name three elements of a proper maintenance schedule for equipment found in commercial kitchens. Use your textbook as a resource.

11. _____

    _____

12. _____

    _____

13. _____

    _____

Using Recipes

12

Culinary Crossword

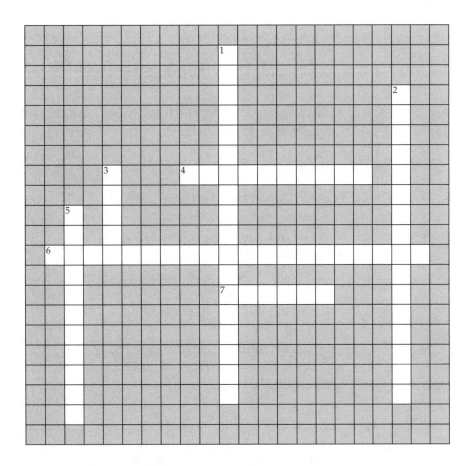

Across

4. Weight of the container that holds the ingredients being measured. (two words)
6. Detailed description of a product used in a foodservice operation. (two words)
7. A list of products and the amounts needed to prepare a dish followed by preparation instructions.

Down

1. Chefs and managers use this tool to create a dish that is uniform each time it is prepared. (two words)
2. A multiplier that adjusts the quantity of each ingredient in the original recipe to determine the quantities needed for the revised recipe. (two words)
3. Term used to describe the quantity or number of portions the recipe will produce.
5. Indicates the serving size that the chef expects to be served to each customer. (two words)

Changing Recipe Yield

Chapter 12

Activity B

Name _____

Date _____ Period _____

To increase or decrease the yield of a recipe, you must accurately adjust the amounts of the ingredients listed in the original recipe. The first step is to determine the conversion factor. The second step is to multiply the amount of each ingredient in the original recipe by that factor.

Part 1: Determine Conversion Factors

Use the following formula to calculate conversion factors.

New Yield ÷ Old Yield = Conversion Factor

Write the equation and solve it to find the conversion factor for each situation below. Round answers two decimal places. (*Reminder: 5 or more rounds up.*)

1. Original recipe makes 12 portions; chef needs 32 portions.

    Equation: _____ Conversion factor = _____

2. Original recipe makes 8 portions; chef needs 64 portions.

    Equation: _____ Conversion factor = _____

3. Original recipe makes 40 portions; chef needs 10 portions.

    Equation: _____ Conversion factor = _____

4. Original recipe makes 20 portions; chef needs 6 portions.

    Equation: _____ Conversion factor = _____

5. Original recipe makes 18 portions; chef needs 126 portions.

    Equation: _____ Conversion factor = _____

(Continued)

Activity B *(Continued)*   **Name** _____

Part 2: Apply Conversion Factors

In the following problems, use the conversion factor to calculate the new quantity needed. Round off answers to two decimal places.

6. Conversion factor is 0.75 and the original quantity is 1 mL.

    New quantity needed = _____

7. Conversion factor is 0.375 and the original quantity is 3 lb.

    New quantity needed = _____

8. Conversion factor is 4.5 and the original quantity is 6 oz.

    New quantity needed = _____

9. Conversion factor is 0.3 and the original quantity is 2.8 L.

    New quantity needed = _____

10. Conversion factor is 6 and the original quantity is 12 eggs.

    New quantity needed = _____

Part 3: Changing Yields

Calculate the following conversions to determine the ingredient amounts needed. Round answers to one decimal place.

11. The original soup recipe calls for 3.5 quarts of stock. The yield is 20 portions. How much stock will be needed to prepare 160 portions? _____

12. The original recipe calls for 7 pounds of veal. The yield is 12 portions. How much veal will be needed for 8 portions? _____

Reviewing Key Concepts

Chapter 12   Name _____

Activity C   Date _____Period_____

Part 1: Measurement and Units of Measure

Complete the list of terms below by writing the abbreviations for the units of measure in the parentheses. Then fill in the blanks in the statements that follow using the appropriate terms from the list. (Some terms will be used more than once, some will not be used at all.)

cup (_____)   liter (_____)   pounds (_____)

fluid ounce (_____)   milliliter (_____)   tablespoon (_____)

gram (_____)   ounces (_____)   volume

kilogram (_____)   pint (_____)   weight

1. Two basic units of weight in the US system of measure are _____ and

   _____.

2. The basic unit of volume in the US system of measure is the _____

   _____.

3. The basic unit of weight in the metric system of measure is the _____.

4. The basic unit of volume in the metric system of measure is the _____.

5. The two units of volume most often used in the metric system are the

   _____ and _____.

6. _____ is the preferred way to measure ingredients in the professional
   kitchen because it is more accurate and consistent than measuring by _____.

7. Water and liquids that have a similar density to water, such as wine, stock, juice, and
   milk, can be measured using either volume or weight. In the US system, one fluid ounce
   of such liquids equals one _____ in weight. In the metric system, one
   milliliter of these liquids equals one _____.

(Continued)

Activity C *(Continued)*   Name _____

Part 2: Equivalents

Write the missing amounts and units in the spaces provided.

8. 1 fluid ounce = _____ mL

9. 1 gallon = 3.8 _____

10. 1 quart = 0.95 _____

11. 1 tablespoon = _____ teaspoons

12. 1 ounce = _____ grams

13. 1 pound = _____ ounces or 454 grams

14. 1 cup = _____ fluid ounces

15. 1 gram = 0.035 _____

Part 3: Standardized Recipes

Read each of the following statements and circle *S* if it describes a standardized recipe. Circle *H* if it is typical of a home recipe.

S   H   16. Ingredients may not be listed separately from the preparation instructions.

S   H   17. Ingredients are always separate from the preparation instructions.

S   H   18. Number of portions may be given, but portion size is not described.

S   H   19. Portion size is expressed in ounces, cups, or by count.

S   H   20. Quantities of most products are measured by weight whenever possible.

S   H   21. Quantities of most products are measured by volume.

S   H   22. Provides detailed product descriptions including market form, size, grade, and brand.

S   H   23. Provides only general, nonspecific names of products.

Part 4: Measuring Accurately

A. Measuring liquid and dry ingredients

Circle the clue in parentheses that best completes each of the following statements.

24. To measure dry ingredients by volume, (**overfill**) (**underfill**) the container and (**scrape off ingredients above the rim**) (**press down ingredients just below the rim**) (**gently shake the container to settle ingredients**).

25. To measure liquid ingredients, (**an opaque**) (**a clear**) container is best. Place the container on a level surface. To read the measurement, bend over so that the measuring line is (**at**) (**just above**) (**just below**) eye level.

(Continued)

Activity C *(Continued)*   **Name** _____

B. Tare weight

Explain how to account for tare weight in each situation below.

26. You must measure out 1½ pounds of sugar. You have a metal bowl to hold the sugar, but the only scale available cannot be reset. How can you adjust for tare weight?

_____

_____

_____

_____

_____

27. You want to measure a quantity of figs in a glass bowl. Your scale can be reset. What steps can you take to determine just the weight of the figs?

_____

_____

_____

Basic Preparations— Mise en Place

Culinary Terminology

Chapter 13

Activity A

Name _____

Date _____ Period_____

Match the following terms and identifying phrases. Terms may be used more than once.

_____ 1. A vegetable-based seasoning made of two parts chopped onion, one part chopped carrot, and one part chopped celery.

_____ 2. Refers to thinly cut strips of leafy greens.

_____ 3. Refers to roughly dicing or chopping a product.

_____ 4. A variation of a vegetable-based seasoning made of three vegetables.

_____ 5. Certain leafy vegetables and fresh herbs can be cut into this.

_____ 6. For even cooking, the three vegetables in this must be cut to the same size.

_____ 7. Is a technique for dicing tomatoes.

_____ 8. Contains two parts chopped onion, one part chopped leek, and one part chopped celery.

_____ 9. Refers to having all foods and equipment ready for a specific preparation before beginning it.

_____ 10. Is ideal for higher temperature cooking.

_____ 11. The fat portion of the butter, which has been separated from the water and milk solids.

_____ 12. Can refer to a state of mental readiness.

A. chiffonade

B. clarified butter

C. concassé

D. mirepoix

E. mise en place

F. white mirepoix

Calculating Butter to Clarified Butter Ratio

Chapter 13

Activity B

Name _____

Date _____Period_____

Clarified butter is one of the staples of professional kitchens. It is ideal for higher temperature cooking. To make clarified butter, you start with whole butter.

A. What makes up butter?

Butter has three basic parts—fat, water, and milk solids. Each part has distinctive properties. Clarified butter is the fat portion.

1. Create a key using a different pattern or color for each part to distinguish among the parts on the graph. In the blank below each key, write the percentage of the whole that each part makes up.

   Key: ☐   Key: ☐   Key: ☐

   _____% Fat   _____% Water   _____% Milk Solids

2. Complete the bar graph below to illustrate the percent each part represents.

B. Calculating quantity of whole butter needed to achieve desired yield.

When butter is clarified, it yields about 75 percent clarified butter. You can use this percentage to calculate how much butter you would need to produce a given amount of clarified butter. For example, if you needed 12 ounces of clarified butter, you would ask the mathematical question: 12 is 75% of what number? Set up this question as an equation in which n represents the unknown quantity of butter needed to produce 12 ounces of clarified butter.

$\frac{12}{n} = \frac{75}{100}$ Cross multiply $\frac{12}{n} \diagdown \frac{75}{100}$ 12 x 100 = n x 75 $1200 = 75n$

Divide both sides by 75 to solve for n $\frac{1200}{75} = \frac{75n}{75}$ 1200 ÷ 75 = n 16 = n

You would need to start with 16 ounces, or 1 pound, of butter to produce 12 ounces of clarified butter. Use this method to calculate how much butter to use to produce the amounts of clarified butter listed below. Show your calculations on a separate sheet of paper. Round answers to nearest whole number.

3. For 10 ounces of clarified butter, begin with_____ of butter.

4. For 18 ounces of clarified butter, begin with_____ of butter.

5. For 170 g of clarified butter, begin with_____of butter.

Reviewing Key Concepts

Chapter 13

Activity C

Name _____

Date _____ Period _____

Part 1: Mise en Place

Place a check (✓) before each element below that is a part of mise en place.

_____ 1. Readying all food and equipment needed for a specific preparation before beginning it.

_____ 2. Setting up your station prior to service.

_____ 3. Chopping herbs and onions.

_____ 4. Getting your mind ready to work.

Part 2: Peeling, Mincing, Dicing, and Julienning Vegetables

Read each statement below. Circle the letter *T* if the statement is true. If the statement is false, circle *F* and write the corrected statement on the lines that follow.

T   F   5.   When peeling an onion, cut the onion horizontally halfway between root and stem.

_____

_____

T   F   6.   To remove the root of an onion make a small triangular cut with tip of a knife.

_____

_____

T   F   7.   To dice onions, be sure the root end of the onion faces away from the knife.

_____

_____

T   F   8.   To peel a garlic clove, lay it on a cutting board, cover with the handle of a chef knife, and press firmly.

_____

_____

T   F   9.   The germ of garlic should be removed if it shows no sign of green.

_____

_____

(Continued)

Activity C *(Continued)*   **Name** _____

T F   10. To mince garlic, begin by coarsely chopping the peeled cloves.

_____

_____

T F   11. To make garlic paste, sprinkle minced garlic with dash of sugar and press with
the side of a knife blade. Repeatedly drag the knife across the garlic.

_____

_____

T F   12. For recipes that rely on a strong parsley flavor, wrung-out parsley works best.

_____

_____

T F   13. To mince parsley, first wash and dry the parsley and then separate the parsley
leaves from the stems.

_____

_____

T F   14. Parsley is wrung out before it is minced.

_____

_____

T F   15. Leeks are unique in that they are dirty on the inside as well as the outside.

_____

_____

T F   16. After trimming the root end of leeks, remove the dark green leaves all at once.

_____

_____

T F   17. For leek halves or quarters, cut leeks in half lengthwise.

_____

_____

(Continued)

Activity C *(Continued)*   **Name** _____

T F   18. To clean leeks, soak them in cold water for 10 to 15 minutes, then pour the leeks
           and soaking water into a colander to drain.

           _____

           _____

T F   19. To peel tomatoes, remove the core, cut an "X" through the skin of the opposite end,
           and plunge in boiling water for 30 seconds. Immediately place in ice water to cool.

           _____

           _____

T F   20. To seed tomatoes, first divide the tomato in half by cutting through the middle.

           _____

           _____

T F   21. Use the concassé technique for dicing tomatoes when you need roughly cut
           tomatoes.

           _____

           _____

T F   22. When preparing a fine dice tomato, the seeds remain inside as the flesh is
           trimmed off.

           _____

           _____

Part 3: Chiffonade Technique

Read each description below and write *Yes* in front of the accurate description and *No* in
front of the inaccurate one.

_____   23. To make a chiffonade, lay five to six leaves side by side on the cutting board. Cut
             across leaves with a sawing motion to make thin slices. Fluff the cuts to reveal
             the chiffonade.

_____   24. To make a chiffonade, lay five to six leaves in a stack on the cutting board.
             Tightly roll the stack. Cut thin slices across the roll. Unroll the cuts to reveal the
             chiffonade.

(Continued)

Activity C *(Continued)*   **Name** _____

Part 4: Clarified Butter

Letter the steps for clarifying butter below in sequential order. The first step should be labeled *A*. Some steps may not be used.

_____ 25. Carefully pour the fat into a clean container.

_____ 26. Ladle remaining fat from the water's surface.

_____ 27. Place butter in metal container.

_____ 28. Place the metal container in lightly simmering water.

_____ 29. Stir after one minute.

_____ 30. Stop pouring when the water becomes visible.

_____ 31. When butter has melted, skim foam off of the top using a ladle.

Kitchen Staples

Culinary Terminology

Name _____

Date _____ Period _____

Match the following terms and identifying phrases.

_____ 1. The green leafy parts of aromatic plants that are used to flavor foods.

_____ 2. The woody parts of plants, including seeds, bark, berries, buds, and roots that are used to flavor foods.

_____ 3. The flavorings or seasonings served with foods to enhance their flavor.

_____ 4. Foods that have been saturated with acid, usually vinegar, in order to preserve them.

_____ 5. Condiment made of a mixture of chopped or diced ingredients preserved in an acidic liquid.

_____ 6. A condiment made of preserved fruits and vegetables with an acidic, sweet and spicy flavor.

_____ 7. The buds of a bush that grows near the Mediterranean.

_____ 8. The fruit of the olive tree that is native to the Mediterranean region.

_____ 9. Small, oily ocean fish preserved by salting.

A. anchovies

B. capers

C. chutney

D. condiments

E. herbs

F. olives

G. pickles

H. relish

I. spices

Reviewing Key Concepts

Chapter 14   Name _____

Activity B   Date _____Period_____

Part 1: Basic Seasonings

Match the following seasonings and identifying phrases. Some seasonings may be used more than once.

_____ 1. Comes from chili peppers.

_____ 2. Is used to season clear broths or consommés because it has no additives.

_____ 3. Not used to season food, but baked shellfish is often served on a bed of it.

_____ 4. Widely used in professional kitchens because it adds pepper flavor without black specks.

_____ 5. The dried berrylike fruit of an Asian plant that is used whole, crushed, cracked, or ground.

_____ 6. Is often referred to as granulated salt because it is in the form of fine granular crystals.

_____ 7. Adds a very strong, hot, spicy flavor to dishes.

_____ 8. Many chefs prefer to use it when sprinkling seasoning with their fingers.

A. black pepper

B. cayenne pepper

C. kosher salt

D. rock salt

E. table salt

F. white pepper

(Continued)

Activity B *(Continued)*   Name _____

Part 2: Herbs

Match the following herbs and identifying phrases. Some herbs may be used more than once.

_____ 9. The classical garnish for fish and poultry.

_____ 10. Often used in pickling and is excellent with fish.

_____ 11. Essential for béarnaise sauce.

_____ 12. Goes well with poultry, pork, and game.

_____ 13. Used in tomato sauces.

_____ 14. Used to flavor stocks, soups, stews, and other savory dishes.

_____ 15. Has a delicate onion-garlic flavor.

_____ 16. Has a strong flavor with citrus tones and is commonly used in salsas.

_____ 17. Also called Italian parsley.

_____ 18. Has a flavor similar to a combination of thyme and oregano.

_____ 19. Garnish for desserts and used with lamb in Middle Eastern cuisines.

_____ 20. Its seeds are a spice called *coriander.*

_____ 21. Has stiff needles on a woody stem and a pinelike aroma.

_____ 22. Is popular in Italian, Greek, and Mexican cuisines and is actually wild marjoram.

_____ 23. Has delicate, lacy leaves with a light licorice flavor and is used in sauces.

A. basil

B. bay leaf

C. chervil

D. chives

E. cilantro

F. dill

G. marjoram

H. mint

I. oregano

J. parsley (curly)

K. parsley (flat-leaf)

L. rosemary

M. sage

N. tarragon

O. thyme

(Continued)

Activity B *(Continued)*   **Name** _____

Part 3: Starches

Match the following starches and identifying phrases. Some starches may be used more than once.

_____ 24. Can be used as a thickening agent.

_____ 25. Can be used as a coating.

_____ 26. Is combined with all-purpose flour to make pasta.

_____ 27. Appropriate for general purpose baking and cooking.

_____ 28. Looks identical to cornstarch.

_____ 29. Lends a light texture to sauces and coatings. Used for tempura batter.

_____ 30. Milled from both yellow and white corn. Used for baking and coating.

_____ 31. Panko is a popular style of this starch.

A. all-purpose flour

B. arrowroot

C. bread crumbs

D. cornmeal

E. cornstarch

F. rice flour

G. semolina

Part 4: Tomato Products

Rank the following tomato products from 1 to 5 in order of the concentration. The product with the greatest concentration should be "1."

_____ tomato juice

_____ tomato paste

_____ tomato purée

_____ fresh tomatoes

_____ tomato sauce

Reviewing Key Concepts

Chapter 14   Name _____

Activity C   Date _____ Period_____

Part 1: Spices

Match the following spices and identifying phrases. Some spices will not be used.

_____	1. The light green, pointed seeds of a plant grown in India that are used in curries, breads, and pastries.
_____	2. Star-shaped fruit of a tree grown in China that is important in Chinese cuisine.
_____	3. Often used in rice dishes, curries, pickling, and prepared mustard, it is known for the bright yellow color it gives dishes.
_____	4. Also known as Jamaican pepper, it is often used in forcemeats, pickling, and baking.
_____	5. Has a strong licorice flavor and is commonly used in liquors and for baking.
_____	6. Dried, bark of a tropical tree with a sweet flavor that makes it popular for use in pastries and fruit dishes.
_____	7. Pale seeds of an annual plant native to India that are used in baked goods and vegetable dishes. The seeds are also ground to a paste to make tahini or pressed to extract oil.
_____	8. Greenish-brown seeds of a plant whose bulb is used as a vegetable. Seeds have a licorice flavor and are often used in sausages and pork dishes.
_____	9. The red, veiny middle layer of the same seed that produces nutmeg with an intense spicy flavor. Used in desserts, baking, and some savory dishes.
_____	10. Seed of an annual plant that originated in the Middle East. Often used in chilies and curries, it is popular in Mexican, Indian, and Middle Eastern cookery.
_____	11. Powder ground from a variety of different red chile peppers.
_____	12. Root of a tropical plant that is used in powdered form for baking, but fresh in Asian cuisines.
_____	13. Berries of an evergreen tree that are used for game dishes and to flavor gin, marinades, and stews.

A. allspice

B. anise

C. caraway seeds

D. cardamom

E. celery seed

F. chile powder

G. cinnamon

H. cloves

I. coriander

J. cumin

K. curry powder

L. dill seed

M. fennel seed

N. ginger

O. juniper berries

P. mace

Q. mustard

R. nutmeg

S. paprika

T. poppy seeds

U. saffron

V. sesame seeds

W. star anise

X. turmeric

(Continued)

Activity C *(Continued)*   **Name** _____

Part 2: Sweeteners

Match the following sweeteners and identifying phrases.

_____ 14. Also known as sucrose, it is primarily used to add a sweet flavor to dishes.

_____ 15. Also known as glucose, its clear form has a neutral sweet flavor; the dark form is more robust.

_____ 16. Graded on color, clarity, and flavor with a light or amber color being most valued.

_____ 17. Created by adding molasses back into refined sugar.

_____ 18. When substituted for sugar gives the dish a distinctive flavor of the sweetener.

_____ 19. The liquid that is leftover after refined sugar is extracted from sugarcane juice.

A. brown sugar

B. corn syrup

C. honey

D. maple syrup

E. molasses

F. sugar

Part 3: Acid Ingredients and Condiments

Read each statement below. Circle the letter *T* if the statement is true. If the statement is false, circle *F* and write the corrected statement on the lines that follow.

T   F   20. Vinegar can be made from any alcoholic beverage.

_____

_____

T   F   21. Malt vinegar is often used as a condiment to baked foods in English cuisine.

_____

_____

T   F   22. The acid content of bottled lemon juice and fresh lemon juice differ widely.

_____

_____

T   F   23. Yellow, or salad style, mustard is a mild mixture. Its color comes from turmeric.

_____

_____

(Continued)

Activity C (*Continued*)   **Name** _____

T   F   24. The flavor of soy sauce is stronger, thicker, and more intense when the ratio of
             wheat to soybeans is high.

_____

_____

T   F   25. Capers should not be rinsed before using them in a recipe.

_____

_____

T   F   26. Chutney is made of preserved fruits and vegetables. It has an acidic, sweet and
             spicy flavor.

_____

_____

T   F   27. Olives are sometimes treated with sugar or vinegar to remove their bitter flavor.

_____

_____

T   F   28. Green olives are picked underripe. Black olives are picked ripe.

_____

_____

T   F   29. Anchovies are mostly sold as fillets canned in water.

_____

_____

T   F   30. The flavor of Worcestershire sauce is derived from dozens of ingredients.

_____

_____

T   F   31. Horseradish's strong burning flavor goes well with rich, fatty meats.

_____

_____

(Continued)

Activity C *(Continued)*   **Name** _____

T   F   32. All hot sauces are basically made from vinegar flavored with sweet peppers and salt.

_____

_____

T   F   33. The most common pickles used in American kitchens are kosher dill pickles, dill gherkins, and cornichons.

_____

_____

Cooking Principles

Culinary Terminology

Name _____

Date _____ Period _____

Part 1

Match the following terms and identifying statements.

_____ 1. The browning that occurs when sugars are heated, resulting in a richer, more complex aroma and flavor.

_____ 2. A cooking method that uses a radiation from a heat source below the food.

_____ 3. To cook food in a liquid at a relatively low temperature.

_____ 4. The process of preparing food for eating by applying heat.

_____ 5. A moist method that cooks a food product by surrounding it with steam vapor.

_____ 6. The manner in which heat energy travels through liquids and gases.

_____ 7. Cooking the food in enough hot fat to cover it half way.

_____ 8. Cooking food in liquid at its highest possible temperature.

_____ 9. Quickly cooking an item in a small amount of hot fat over high heat.

_____ 10. Cooking process that combines browning and simmering.

_____ 11. Process during which starches combine with hot liquid and absorb the liquid and swell.

A. boiling

B. braising

C. caramelization

D. convection

E. cooking

F. gelatinization

G. grilling

H. panfrying

I. poach

J. sautéing

K. steaming

(Continued)

Activity A *(Continued)*   **Name** _____

Part 2

_____ 12. To brown a food product. Often described by the French term *au gratin*.

_____ 13. The method that cooks a food by surrounding it with hot air.

_____ 14. Cooking food in a small amount of fat using low heat in order to soften the food without browning.

_____ 15. A method that cooks food in enough hot fat to fully cover the item.

_____ 16. Cooking food in liquid at a temperature just below boiling.

_____ 17. Cooking by using a radiant heat source located above the food.

_____ 18. The transfer of heat energy from one object to another through direct contact.

_____ 19. The method used to cook foods in the oven with a certain amount of added moisture.

_____ 20. The transfer of heat energy through waves.

A. baking

B. broiling

C. conduction

D. deep frying

E. gratiner

F. radiation

G. roasting

H. simmering

I. sweating

The Science of Cooking

Chapter 15

Activity B

Name _____

Date _____ Period _____

Part 1: The Chemistry of Cooking

Select the appropriate phrases from the following list to complete the chart below. Place the letter for each phrase in the appropriate box.

Chemical Changes Resulting from Cooking

A. Much of the connective tissue in meat becomes tender when it is properly cooked.

B. Heat causes sugars to caramelize.

C. Starches combine with hot liquid, and swell in a process called gelatinization.

D. The cell structure of most plants is broken down by heat.

E. When proteins are heated, they coagulate.

F. Amino acids, which make up proteins, change when heated, creating new flavors.

G. Most bacteria, fungi, and molds are killed at normal cooking temperatures.

H. Applying heat blends the flavors of multiple ingredients.

Cooking Chemistry	
Reasons for Cooking Foods	**Chemical Changes Resulting from Cooking**
Cooked food is safer to eat.	
Cooked food is more digestible.	
Cooking improves texture, taste, aroma, and appearance of food.	

Identify what can happen when foods are cooked to excessive temperatures or for too long by completing the following statements on the lines provided.

1. When food is overcooked, nutrients are _____ .

2. When food is overcooked, sugars burn causing foods to taste _____ .

3. When food is overcooked, moisture is lost and foods become _____ .

4. When food is overcooked, proteins can _____ or _____ .

5. When food is overcooked, texture is destroyed and foods become either
_____ or _____ .

6. When food is overcooked, the color of green vegetables _____ .

(Continued)

Activity B *(Continued)*   **Name** _____

Part 2: The Physics of Cooking

Circle the clue in parentheses that best completes each of the following statements.

7. The transfer of heat energy through waves is referred to as (**conduction**) (**convection**) (**radiation**).

8. The transfer of heat energy from one object to another through direct contact is referred to as (**conduction**) (**convection**) (**radiation**).

9. The transfer of heat energy through liquids and gases is referred to as (**conduction**) (**convection**) (**radiation**).

10. The flames of a broiler transferring heat to food being cooked is an example of heat transfer by (**conduction**) (**convection**) (**radiation**).

11. A pot of boiling liquid being stirred is an example of heat transfer by (**conduction**) (**convection**) (**radiation**).

12. Microwaves also cook food by (**conduction**) (**convection**) (**radiation**).

13. Food cooking in a pan on a range is an example of heat transfer by (**conduction**) (**convection**) (**radiation**).

14. The natural rising of warm air to the top of an oven and the descending of the cooler air to the bottom of the oven is an example of heat transfer by (**conduction**) (**convection**) (**radiation**).

Cooking Methods

Chapter 15

Activity C

Name _____

Date _____ Period _____

For each cooking example given in the chart, select the appropriate cooking method from the list below and write it in the middle column. In the last column, circle the correct classification—**dry heat method (DHM), moist heat method (MHM), combination method (CM)**—for that cooking method.

Cooking Methods

baking	deep frying	poaching	simmering
boiling	grilling	roasting	steaming
braising	panfrying	sautéing	stewing
broiling			

Cooking Methods		
Cooking Example	**Cooking Method**	**Classification** *(Circle one)*
Food is browned on all sides in fat, then liquid is added and food is simmered.		(DHM) (MHM) (CM)
Food is quickly cooked in a small amount of hot fat over high heat.		(DHM) (MHM) (CM)
Food is cooked in enough hot fat to fully cover the food item.		(DHM) (MHM) (CM)
Food is cooked by surrounding it with steam vapor.		(DHM) (MHM) (CM)
Food is cooked in enough hot fat to cover the food item halfway.		(DHM) (MHM) (CM)
Food is cut in small pieces and cooked in enough liquid for them to float freely during the process.		(DHM) (MHM) (CM)
Some moisture is added to food and then it is cooked in the oven.		(DHM) (MHM) (CM)
Food is cooked by surrounding it with hot air.		(DHM) (MHM) (CM)
Food to be cooked is placed on a pan or a grill and then placed under the heat source.		(DHM) (MHM) (CM)
Food is cooked over a heat source.		(DHM) (MHM) (CM)
Food is cooked in liquid at a temperature just below boiling.		(DHM) (MHM) (CM)
Food is cooked in a liquid at a relatively low temperature.		(DHM) (MHM) (CM)
Food is cooked in liquid at its highest possible temperature.		(DHM) (MHM) (CM)

Salads and Dressings

Culinary Terminology

Name _____

Date _____ Period_____

Match the following terms and identifying phrases. Some terms may be used more than once.

_____ 1. Usually made up of four parts—base, body, dressing, and garnish.

_____ 2. When cooked items are mixed with mayonnaise.

_____ 3. A salad of greens and various raw vegetables such as cucumbers, carrots, and tomatoes.

_____ 4. A mixture of three parts oil to one part vinegar.

_____ 5. A cold sauce that is an emulsion of oil and vinegar stabilized with egg yolk and mustard.

_____ 6. Also known as a plated salad.

_____ 7. May be served with any kind of dressing, which can be either tossed with the salad or served on the side.

_____ 8. Cooked foods mixed with a vinaigrette.

_____ 9. A mixture of baby lettuces.

_____ 10. A mixture of two liquids that don't naturally mix, such as oil and vinegar.

_____ 11. Important in the cold kitchen because it is often used as a base for dressings or cold sauces.

_____ 12. Made up of tiny droplets of one ingredient suspended in another ingredient.

A. bound salad

B. composed salad

C. emulsion

D. marinated salad

E. mayonnaise

F. mesclun

G. simple salad

H. vinaigrette

Identifying Salads and Their Ingredients

Chapter 16

Name _____

Activity B

Date _____ Period _____

Part 1: Types of Salads on the Menu

Circle the clue in parentheses that best completes each of the following statements.

1. The traditional purpose salads have served on the menu is as (**an entrée**) (**an appetizer**) (**a dessert**).

2. Green salad paired with portions of cooked chicken, seafood, or meat is an example of (**an appetizer salad**) (**a main course salad**) (**a bar salad**).

3. Restaurant operators like salad bars because ingredient costs are relatively (**high**) (**low**) and labor costs are (**increased**) (**decreased**).

4. When salad ingredients are assembled in a particular arrangement, the finished salad is a (**simple salad**) (**composed salad**) (**bound salad**) (**marinated salad**).

5. A salad of greens and various raw vegetables such as cucumbers, carrots, and tomatoes is a (**simple salad**) (**composed salad**) (**bound salad**) (**marinated salad**).

6. A plated salad is also called a (**simple salad**) (**composed salad**) (**bound salad**) (**marinated salad**).

7. When cooked items are mixed with mayonnaise, they are referred to as (**simple salad**) (**composed salad**) (**bound salad**) (**marinated salad**).

8. Regardless of the ingredients, a (**simple salad**) (**composed salad**) (**bound salad**) (**marinated salad**) usually includes the following four parts: base, body, dressing, garnish.

9. When cooked foods are mixed with a vinaigrette, they are commonly called a (**simple salad**) (**composed salad**) (**bound salad**) (**marinated salad**).

10. Tossing simple salads with dressing too (**forcefully**) (**far in advance**) (**gently**) will cause the salad greens to wilt.

(Continued)

Activity B *(Continued)*   **Name** _____

Part 2: Salad Greens

Match the following salad greens with the identifying phrases.

_____ 11. Soft green leaves form a loose head with creamy-colored inner leaves. The leaves have a delicate texture and cupped shape.

_____ 12. Tightly packed, elongated head of white leaves with yellow tips and a bitter flavor.

_____ 13. Red lettuce with white stems and veins, and a bitter flavor.

_____ 14. Tender little shoots of various plants such as alfalfa, mung beans, radishes, and mustard.

_____ 15. Large, tender, ruffled bunches of bright green leaves with a mild flavor. Used in salads, sandwiches, and for lining plates and platters.

_____ 16. Developed in Kentucky, this lettuce has color and texture similar to Boston lettuce but forms a smaller head. One whole head is often served as a single portion.

_____ 17. With crisp leaves and round shape, this is the most popular variety of lettuce in the United States.

_____ 18. This loosely formed head of flat, curly edged leaves that are dark green at the tip and yellowish white at the base is often prepared as a hot vegetable in Italian cuisine.

_____ 19. With an elongated, tightly packed head with round-tipped leaves and crisp ribs, it is the second most popular lettuce in the United States.

_____ 20. A mixture of baby lettuces that is often purchased cut, washed, mixed, and ready to use.

_____ 21. Can be purchased in bunches or cello pack. Fibrous stems should be removed and leaves washed several times, however, the smaller, tender leaves are best for salads.

_____ 22. Has the same texture and flavor as green leaf lettuce but with reddish-brown color at the tip of the leaves.

_____ 23. The classic plate garnish for red meats, but also used in salads. Has a peppery flavor.

_____ 24. Crisp ribs create narrow leaves with a curly edge. Outer leaves are deep green with a pale yellow core. It has a bitter flavor and is usually served as part of a mix.

A. Belgian endive

B. bibb lettuce

C. Boston lettuce

D. curly endive

E. escarole

F. iceberg lettuce

G. leaf lettuce

H. mesclun

I. radicchio

J. red leaf lettuce

K. romaine lettuce

L. spinach

M. sprouts

N. watercress

Purchase and Preparation

Chapter 16

Activity C

Name _____

Date _____ Period _____

Part 1: Buying Lettuce

Circle the clue in parentheses that best completes each of the following statements.

1. Compared to other produce, lettuce is (**more**) (**less**) subject to fluctuations in quality and price.

2. Produce wholesalers generally sell lettuce by (**weight**) (**head**).

3. The waste from trimming or damaged leaves (**affects**) (**does not affect**) cost.

4. The lowest priced lettuce is (**always**) (**never**) (**not always**) the best buy.

5. The cost of ready-to-eat greens is (**lower**) (**higher**) than traditional greens.

6. Using ready-to-eat greens results in (**more prep time but less waste**) (**less prep time but more waste**) (**less prep time and less waste**).

Part 2: Preparing Salad Greens

Read each statement below. Circle the letter *T* if the statement is true. If the statement is false, circle *F* and write the corrected statement on the lines that follow.

T   F   7.   In a commercial kitchen, lettuce and greens are washed under running water.

_____

_____

T   F   8.   The cores on head lettuce and the thick stems on leafy greens should be removed.

_____

_____

T   F   9.   The best method for drying greens is to pat them with absorbent paper towel.

_____

_____

(Continued)

Activity C (*Continued*)   **Name** _____

T   F   10. Because cutting lettuce with most knives causes oxidation, lettuce should always
             be torn, never cut.

_____

_____

T   F   11. Wilted, outer leaves should be removed and discarded.

_____

_____

T   F   12. In most cases, lettuce leaves should be kept whole for salads.

_____

_____

Part 3: Dressings and Salad Preparation

Circle the clue in parentheses that best completes each of the following statements.

13. In vinaigrette, the task of the acidic vinegar is to (**enhance**) (**cut**) (**dissolve**) the fat, add
    another taste sensation, and (**help**) (**stop**) the oil from coating the palate.

14. The secret to preparing a good vinaigrette is balance between fat, acid, and other
    seasonings. The best ratio is usually (**two parts vinegar to one part oil**) (**one part oil to
    one part vinegar**) (**three parts oil to one part vinegar**) by volume.

15. It is important to stir simple vinaigrette (**well**) (**immediately**) before servings.

16. An emulsion is a mixture of two liquids that (**don't naturally**) (**naturally and easily**) mix.

17. Adding egg or egg yolk to mayonnaise (**separates**) (**stabilizes**) oil and vinegar.

18. The standard proportion for making mayonnaise is (**one half**) (**one**) (**one and one half**)
    egg yolk to (**one half**) (**one**) (**one and one half**) cup of oil.

19. The consistency of most emulsified dressings is (**thicker than**) (**thinner than**)
    (**about the same as**) mayonnaise.

20. The ingredient that makes up the biggest percent of most salad dressings is (**vinegar**)
    (**oil**) (**spices**).

21. The source of a particular oil, vinegar, or mustard (**can**) (**cannot**) noticeably alter the
    flavor of a salad dressing.

(Continued)

Activity C *(Continued)*   **Name** _____

22. Mustard helps to (**separate**) (**cut**) (**emulsify**) mayonnaise and other emulsified dressings.

23. One yolk is roughly equivalent to (**one fluid ounce**) (**one tablespoon**) of pasteurized egg products, which are commonly used in commercial kitchens.

24. Keeping salad ingredients (**chilled**) (**at room temperature**) helps keep them sanitary.

25. (**Warm**) (**Chill**) salad plates before plating to avoid (**wilting**) (**frosting**) greens.

26. Use gloves or utensils to handle salad ingredients because it is (**unstable**) (**ready-to-eat**) food.

27. Mix tossed salads with dressing (**as close to service as possible**) (**as early as possible before service**).

28. When applying salad dressings, the rule is use just enough to (**cover the bottom of the bowl**) (**lightly coat the greens**).

Fruit Identification

Culinary Terminology

Name _____

Date _____ Period _____

Match the following terms and identifying phrases.

Part 1

_____ 1. The weight of the packaging alone.

_____ 2. Same grade as *Choice* for canned or frozen fruits.

_____ 3. A volume measuring 35.24 liters or about 2200 cubic inches.

_____ 4. The total weight of a container and the product.

_____ 5. A large bulk-packed case.

_____ 6. A box or container of varying size. May be made of cardboard, wood, plastic, or foam.

_____ 7. Equivalent to one-fourth bushel.

_____ 8. Same grade as *Fancy* for canned or frozen fruits.

_____ 9. A specific number of pieces of uniform-sized produce in a case or container.

_____ 10. The weight of the product without the packaging.

A. bushel

B. case

C. count

D. gross weight

E. lug

F. net weight

G. peck

H. tare weight

I. US Grade A

J. US Grade B

(Continued)

Activity A *(Continued)*   **Name** _____

Part 2

_____ 11. A shallow single-layered case used for delicate products such as berries and figs.

_____ 12. A wooden case.

_____ 13. Same grade as *Standard* for canned or frozen fruits.

_____ 14. Evaluating a food against a uniform set of quality standards.

_____ 15. The federal agency that imposes standards for the quality and safety of food products in the United States.

A. crate

B. flat

C. grading

D. USDA

E. US Grade C

Identifying Quality Fruits

Chapter 17

Activity B

Name _____

Date _____Period_____

Part 1: Identifying Fruits

Circle the clue in parentheses that best completes each of the following statements.

1. Oranges named for the navel-like protrusion near their stem are (**Valencia**) (**navel**) (**blood**).

2. The most important variety of orange is (**Valencia**) (**navel**) (**blood**).

3. Citrus fruits named for the deep red color of their flesh are (**tangerines**) (**blood oranges**).

4. Grapefruit fall into one of two categories based on (**flavor**) (**the color of their flesh**).

5. The most popular variety of apple in the United States is (**Fuji**) (**Gala**) (**Red Delicious**).

6. (**Braeburn**) (**Golden Delicious**) (**Cortland**) is *not* an all purpose apple.

7. Northern Spy, Spartan, and Granny Smith are (**cooking**) (**eating**) (**all purpose**) apples.

8. (**Seckel**) (**Asian**) (**Anjou**) are sweet, firm, crisp, and fragrant round shaped pears.

9. Cherries are classified into two main categories: (**light and dark**) (**sweet and sour**).

10. (**Bing**) (**Rainier**) (**Montmorency**) cherries are noted for bright red skin and juicy fruit.

11. The classification of peaches is based on (**color**) (**how difficult it is to remove their pits**).

12. A nectarine is a (**fuzzless peach**) (**type of stone fruit**) (**cross of a peach and a plum**).

13. Pound for pound, berries are among the (**cheapest**) (**most expensive**) fruits.

14. Tiny red seedless grapes that form in long clusters are (**Ribier**) (**Corinth**) (**Concord**) grapes.

15. The three melons commonly used in the commercial kitchen are (**Crenshaw, casaba, and cantaloupe**) (**honeydew, watermelon, and cantaloupe**) (**watermelon, casaba, and cantaloupe**).

16. The (**Cavendish**) (**plantain**) (**finger**) banana is the most common variety eaten in the United States.

17. Calimyrna, Mission, and Kadota are the most popular variety of (**kiwifruit**) (**figs**) (**dates**).

18. A small brown-skinned fruit that has a white inner flesh with sweet, juicy, subtle flavor; originally grown in China is the (**kumquat**) (**lychee**) (**Kiwano**).

19. An oval fruit that looks like a five point star when sliced is (**carambola**) (**cherimoya**).

20. A small thumb-sized citrus fruit with almost no juice is (**kumquat**) (**lychee**) (**kiwano**).

(Continued)

Activity B *(Continued)*   **Name** _____

Part 2: Quality Factors for Selection

Circle the clue in parentheses that best completes each of the following statements.

21. (**Heavier**) (**Lighter**) citrus fruit generally has greater juice content.

22. (**Smooth**) (**Bumpy**) -skinned oranges are easier to peel and best for eating out of hand.

23. (**Smooth**) (**Bumpy**) -skinned oranges are hard to peel and reserved for juicing.

24. Green spots on grapefruit skin (**are**) (**are not**) a sign that the fruit is unripe.

25. When buying lemons look for (**fine-textured**) (**rough-textured**) skin and relatively (**light**) (**heavy**) weight for their size.

26. In lemons, (**deep**) (**light**) yellow color is a sign of maturity and (**less**) (**more**) acid.

27. Select apples that feel (**soft**) (**firm**) to the touch and have color appropriate for the variety.

28. For cooking, baking, and applesauce choose (**sweet, soft fleshed**) (**firm, tart**) apples.

29. For eating choose (**sweet, soft-fleshed**) (**firm, tart**) apples.

30. Ripe pears should (**resist slightly**) (**yield slightly**) to a gentle squeeze.

31. Many chefs prefer to buy pears (**fully ripened on the tree**) (**immature to ripen themselves**).

32. When choosing apricots, choose fruit that is (**green**) (**yellow**) and (**hard**) (**slightly soft**).

33. Quality peaches (**should**) (**should not**) have a fragrant aroma.

34. The deep red on orange color of nectarines (**is**) (**is not**) a sign of ripeness.

35. Plums should have good color for their variety and (**resist**) (**yield**) slightly to pressure.

36. Berries should be (**soft**) (**firm**) and (**bright**) (**even**) colored.

37. Juice stains at the bottom of the berry container are a sign that the berries are (**ripe**) (**deteriorating**).

38. Select cranberries with bright red color and a (**hard**) (**soft**) (**springy**) texture.

39. Select (**compact**) (**loose**) bunches of grapes with (**moist, pliable**) (**dry, brittle**) stems.

40. Ripeness in cantaloupe (**can**) (**cannot**) be determined by its fragrance.

41. Regardless of the color of the outer rind, the best sign of watermelon ripeness is a pale (**green**) (**yellow**) underside.

42. Ripe papayas have skin that is at least half (**yellow**) (**red**).

43. The only sure way to determine pineapple ripeness is to (**squeeze**) (**taste**) them.

44. Persimmons are rather (**soft**) (**firm**) when ripe.

45. Fragrance (**is**) (**is not**) a sign of ripeness in persimmons.

Fresh in Season or Processed?

Chapter 17

Activity C

Name _____

Date _____Period_____

Part 1: Seasons for Fresh Fruits

Next to each month in the chart below, write the letters of every fruit that is in season during that period.

A. apricots

B. Bartlett pears

C. blackberries

D. blood oranges

E. blueberries

F. cherries

G. Cortland apples

H. cranberries

I. currents

J. figs

K. Gala apples

L. Granny Smith apples

M. honeydew melons

N. lemons

O. McIntosh apples

P. navel oranges

Q. papaya

R. peaches

S. pineapples

T. plums

U. raspberries

V. Rome Beauty apples

W. strawberries

X. Valencia oranges

Month	Fruits in Season
January	
February	
March	
April	
May	
June	
July	
August	
September	
October	
November	
December	

(Continued)

Activity C *(Continued)*   **Name** _____

Part 2: Drying Fruits

Circle the clue in parentheses that best completes each of the following statements.

1. Raisins are dried (**grapes**) (**green grapes**) (**plums**) (**currents**).

2. Prunes are dried (**grapes**) (**green grapes**) (**plums**) (**currents**).

3. Sultanas are dried (**grapes**) (**green grapes**) (**plums**) (**currents**).

4. Some dried fruits are treated with (**carbon dioxide**) (**sulfur dioxide**) to preserve their color and stop spoilage.

5. Keep dried fruits in (**an open**) (**a sealed**) container to preserve their flavor.

6. Many dried fruits are rehydrated or (**warmed**) (**moistened**) before using.

Part 3: Canned Fruits

Circle the clue in parentheses that best completes each of the following statements.

7. The flavor of canned fruits is usually consistent all year long because the fruits are usually packed at the (**beginning**) (**peak**) (**end**) of the season.

8. Fruit packed in (**water**) (**syrup**) retains more of the natural flavors of the fruit.

9. Fruit packed in (**water**) (**syrup**) is less likely to be broken or crushed.

10. The canning process preserves foods from spoilage until the can is opened and (**the fruit begins to dry**) (**the vacuum is broken**).

Part 4: Frozen Fruits

Circle the clue in parentheses that best completes each of the following statements.

11. Frozen fruits retain (**more**) (**less**) flavor of fresh fruit than dry fruit retains.

12. Individually quick frozen (IQF) fruits are flash frozen (**before**) (**after**) packing and they tend to (**lose**) (**retain**) their original shape.

13. Adding sugar adds flavor and keeps fruit (**fully frozen**) (**from fully freezing**).

Fruit Preparation

Culinary Terminology

Chapter 18

Activity A

Name _____

Date _____ Period _____

Match the following terms and identifying phrases. Then, circle the clue in parentheses that best completes the description.

_____ 1. A decoration added to a dish to make it (**sanitary**) (**attractive**).

_____ 2. The white, spongy inner part of (**citrus**) (**acidulating**) fruits.

_____ 3. Briefly cooking an item in (**simmering**) (**boiling**) water.

_____ 4. The process of (**adding acid to**) (**removing acid from**) an item.

_____ 5. To reconstitute or return some of the liquid removed from the fruit in the (**cooking**) (**preparation**) (**drying**) process.

_____ 6. The browning of (**all**) (**certain**) fruits once they are cut and exposed to the air.

_____ 7. The colorful, outermost part of the skin of (**citrus**) (**acidulating**) fruits.

_____ 8. An individual segment of any citrus fruit (**with**) (**without**) skin, pith, seeds, or membrane.

A. acidulation

B. blanching

C. garnish

D. oxidation

E. pith

F. plumping

G. suprême

H. zest

Preparing Fruit

Chapter 18   Name _____

Activity B   Date _____ Period _____

Match each fruit group to the preparation technique that is most appropriate.

A. apples and pears

B. apples, pears, bananas, avocados

C. apples, pears, mangoes, and papayas

D. berries

E. cherries

F. citrus fruits

G. melons

H. melons, pineapples, citrus fruits, and kiwis

I. peaches, nectarines, and plums

J. peaches and nectarines

K. pineapples

1. _____

Peeling and Coring

- Cut off the top and bottom.
- Trim the skin following the contour of the fruit from top to bottom.
- Continue working around the fruit until the skin is removed.
- Remove the eyes.
- Cut the fruit in quarters lengthwise.
- Cut away from the fibrous core.

2. _____

Coring

- Using a knife, cut the fruit in quarters through the stem.
- Cut out the core and seeds with a knife.
- Continue to cut into smaller pieces if desired.

3. _____

Washing

- Gently submerge in cold water.
- Drain.
- Wash as close to time of service as possible to avoid fruit getting mushy.

4. _____

Zesting

- Use a special tool called a zester to remove the outermost part of the fruit skin in fine julienne strips.
- If a zester is not available, use a peeler or a grater to remove the outermost part of the skin.

5. _____

Acidulating

- Dip or brush cut fruit with one tablespoon of lemon juice to one quart of water.
- Dip rather then soak the fruit.

(Continued)

Activity B *(Continued)*   Name _____

6. _____

Removing Skin by Blanching
- Drop into rapidly boiling water for a few moments.
- Place in cold water to cool down.

7. _____

Removing Skin with Knife
- Use utility knife or flexible boning knife to remove skin.
- Cut as little of the flesh as possible. Fruits should retain their rounded shape.

8. _____

Peeling and Seeding
- Using a flexible knife, cut off the top and bottom.
- Using a slicing motion, trim the skin following the contour of the fruit from top to bottom.
- Continue trimming around the fruit until all the skin and rind is removed.
- Cut the peeled fruit in half and scrape out the seeds with a spoon.

9. _____

Removing Skin with a Peeler
- Use a stationary or swivel peeler to remove skin.

10. _____

Pitting
- Use a paring knife and cut through the skin and flesh to the pit.
- Cut to the pit a full 360 degrees.
- Gently twist the two halves of the fruit in opposite directions until they separate.
- Use the tip of a paring knife to remove the pit from the fruit.

11. _____

Pitting
- Using the special tool designed for the purpose, push the pit through the flesh.
- The fruit should remain uncrushed.

Fruit Presentation and Cooking

Chapter 18

Activity C

Name _____

Date _____ Period _____

Part 1: Preparing Fruit Garnishes

Circle the clue in parentheses that best completes each of the following statements.

A. Parisiennes and citrus slices

1. The tool used to make Parisiennes is sometimes called a (**melon baller**) (**melon scoop**). Carve out each additional Parisienne (**close to**) (**far from**) the previous one to (**protect its shape**) (**minimize waste**).

2. Citrus slices can be made more interesting by cutting channels (**parallel**) (**perpendicular**) to the direction the slices will be cut. This exposes alternating stripes of white (**pith**) (**flesh**) and colorful (**flesh**) (**zest**) once the fruit is cut into thin slices.

3. Citrus slices can be turned into twists by cutting the slice from center to the outer edge and bending the halves in the (**same**) (**opposite**) direction.

B. Fruit crowns

4. Grip a paring knife on the blade that is at a point that is about the length of the (**diameter**) (**radius**) of the piece of fruit.

5. Hold the knife at a 45°angle to an imaginary line around the (**top**) (**middle**) (**bottom**) of the fruit. Insert the tip of the knife and push in until it reaches the center.

6. Hold the knife at (**a similar**) (**an opposing**) 45° angle and make a cut adjacent to the first one. Make sure the cuts (**overlap**) (**do not overlap**).

7. Continue these zigzag cuts around the fruit until you reach the starting point. Each cut (**should always**) (**should never**) intersect its adjacent cuts. Pull halves apart.

C. Fruit fans

8. To make a fruit fan, begin by cutting a (**flat**) (**rounded**) side on the bottom of a piece of fruit. Make a slice at a (**45°**) (**90°**) angle to the cutting board. Cut through all but a small portion of the fruit.

9. Make additional slices (**parallel**) (**perpendicular**) to the first slice making sure to (**never**) (**always**) cut all the way through.

10. Press on the piece of fruit in the (**opposite**) (**same**) direction as the slices to open the fan.

(Continued)

Activity C *(Continued)*   **Name** _____

Part 2: Cooking Fruit

Read each statement below. Circle the letter *T* if the statement is true. If the statement is false, circle *F* and write the corrected statement on the lines that follow.

T   F   11. Fruits can be poached, steamed, or fried, but should never be baked, grilled, or sautéed.

_____

_____

T   F   12. The cooking process preserves the fruit's rigid cell structure.

_____

_____

T   F   13. The degree of ripeness affects cooking time.

_____

_____

T   F   14. In general, cooked fruits should still be firm when pierced with a fork or tip of a knife.

_____

_____

T   F   15. Dried fruits are plumped to return some of the liquid removed from the fruit in the drying process.

_____

_____

T   F   16. Plumping is done by soaking the dried fruit in cold liquid or simmering them in liquid.

_____

_____

Notes

Cold Sandwiches 19

Culinary Terminology

Chapter 19

Activity A

Name _____

Date _____ Period _____

Circle the clue in parentheses that best completes each of the following statements.

1. (**À la Carte**) (**Baguette**) (**Pullman loaf**) is bread that is finely textured and cuts into square slices.

2. A preparation that involves a number of ingredients placed on, in, or between bread is referred to as a (**canapé**) (**Pullman loaf**) (**sandwich**).

3. The most common rolled sandwich today is the (**à la carte**) (**canapé**) (**wrap**).

4. A system in which food is prepared only when an order is received from the service staff is referred to as preparing food (**à la carte**) (**Danish sandwich**) (**baguette**).

5. Various ingredients rolled in a tortilla are called a (**canapé**) (**finger sandwich**) (**wrap**).

6. A category of sandwiches that includes tea sandwiches is (**à la carte**) (**finger sandwiches**) (**canapé**).

7. (**À la carte**) (**Danish sandwich**) (**Canapé**) sandwich stations are designed with speed in mind.

8. (**Baguette**) (**Pullman loaf**) (**Finger sandwich**) is the name for a long, thin French bread.

9. Neat, open-faced sandwiches that often include strongly flavored foods are referred to as (**Danish sandwiches**) (**finger sandwiches**) (**tea sandwiches**).

10. Small, bite-size, well-garnished, and attractive hors d'oeuvres that come in many different forms are referred to as (**à la carte**) (**canapés**) (**finger sandwiches**).

11. (**Canapé**) (**Danish sandwiches**) (**Tea sandwiches**) are small, closed-faced sandwiches made with crustless bread and trimmed to neat shapes.

12. A (**baguette**) (**Pullman loaf**) (**wrap**) is baked inside a mold with a cover.

Sandwich Types and Attributes

Chapter 19   Name _____

Activity B   Date _____ Period _____

Part 1: Types of Sandwiches

List the five types of sandwiches in alphabetical order on the lines lettered A through E. Then, match the sandwich types with the identifying phrases.

_____ 1. After soft white bread has been flattened with a rolling pin, ingredients are then rolled tightly in the flattened bread.

A. _____

B _____

_____ 2. A single slice of a small-diameter loaf of rye bread is spread with cream cheese and neatly topped with smoked salmon.

C. _____

D. _____

_____ 3. A bite-sized round of bread buttered and topped with a thin slice of cucumber.

E. _____

_____ 4. A club sandwich.

_____ 5. A single slice of whole-grain bread is topped with lettuce and thin slices of avocado then sprinkled with lemon juice.

Part 2: Attributes of Sandwiches

Chapter 19 names five attributes of successful and delicious sandwiches. Complete the following chart with the name of the attribute that corresponds to each of the chef's sandwich-making choices.

Chef's Sandwich Making Choices	Sandwich Attribute Achieved
6. Carefully spread the bread thinly with mayonnaise and lightly drizzle top of sandwich ingredients with olive oil.	
7. Lightly sprinkle the top layer of ingredients with finely minced ripe tomatoes and green pepper.	
8. Placed ingredients neatly and precisely on the bread making sure that the ingredients would not fall out when the sandwich was held.	
9. Selected strongly flavored condiments and ripe vegetables to add to the sandwich ingredients.	
10. Topped soft cheese with thin slices of crisp radish.	

Sandwich Ingredients and Assembly

Chapter 19

Activity C

Name _____

Date _____ Period_____

Part 1: Sandwich Ingredients

Read each statement below. Circle the letter *T* if the statement is true. If the statement is false, circle *F* and write the corrected statement on the lines that follow.

T   F   1.   All sandwiches include some type of bread.

_____

_____

T   F   2.   Type of bread is always a choice regardless of the type of sandwich.

_____

_____

T   F   3.   Sturdy, country-style loaves are ideal for delicate sandwiches like tea sandwiches.

_____

_____

T   F   4.   Originally served as breakfast rolls in France, focaccia are light crescent-shaped rolls that are often used for sandwiches today.

_____

_____

T   F   5.   Spreads prevent wet fillings from soaking into the bread because they are high in fat.

_____

_____

T   F   6.   Bound salad sandwiches do not need a spread.

_____

_____

T   F   7.   Sandwiches are usually named after the bread rather than the filling.

_____

_____

Activity C (*Continued*)   **Name** _____

T   F   8.   Many sandwich fillings are high carbohydrate ingredients, which means
             sanitation practices must be rigorously followed when preparing sandwiches.

_____

_____

T   F   9.   Cheeses can add moisture as well as flavor and texture to a sandwich.

_____

_____

T   F   10. Garnishes need to look good, but flavor is usually not important.

_____

_____

Part 2: Sandwich Assembly

A. Sandwich assembly strategies

Circle the clue in parentheses that best completes each of the following statements.

11. À la carte assembly strategies are also called (**self-serve**) (**made to order**).

12. In an à la carte assembly, all sandwich ingredients should be (**nearby**) (**within easy reach**).

13. À la carte sandwich stations should have a consistent (**alternating**) (**linear**) workflow.

14. In an à la carte sandwich station, the cutting board should be (**compact so as to not take
     up too much room**) (**large enough to hold several sandwiches at a time**).

15. Preportioned ingredients (**have no place**) (**save valuable time**) in an à la carte sandwich
     station.

16. Sandwich bars constitute a type of buffet because (**customers serve themselves**)
     (**customers selections are made to order**).

17. Sneeze guards are recommended for (**aesthetic**) (**health**) reasons.

18. Sandwich bars have become increasingly popular (**dinner**) (**lunch**) options.

19. Sandwich bars should be (**kept stocked**) (**replenished only during peak times**).

(Continued)

Activity C *(Continued)*   **Name** _____

B. Sandwich assembly line

In the spaces provided, briefly describe what tasks each person in a five-station assembly line might perform to prepare a closed sandwich with mayonnaise, lettuce, cheese, cucumbers, minced olives, and mustard. The finished sandwich is wrapped in plastic and boxed.

Assembly Line Workers	Sandwich Assembly Tasks
20. First person	
21. Second person	
22. Third person	
23. Fourth person	
24. Fifth person	

Notes

Stocks

Culinary Crossword

Name _____

Date _____ Period _____

Across

1. A concentrated instant powder or paste that dissolves in hot water to make a stocklike liquid.

2. One of two names for stocklike preparations that are made with a larger proportion of meat than bone and a greater variety of vegetables.

3. An animal protein that when dissolved in a hot liquid adds to a rich mouthfeel.

6. A bundle of fresh herbs tied to a piece of celery, leek, or carrot. (two words)

9. Dissolving the browned bits off the bottom of pan when preparing brown stock.

10. A highly flavored liquid made by simmering bones with vegetables, herbs, and spices.

Down

1. Stock made from roasted bones and roasted or sautéed mirepoix. (two words)

4. The process of placing bones in cold water, bringing the water to a boil, and then discarding water.

5. Stocks made using poultry, fish, or veal bones. (two words)

6. One of two names for stocklike preparations that are made with a larger proportion of meat than bone and a greater variety of vegetables.

7. French name for fish stock.

8. A small cheesecloth bag containing herbs and spices.

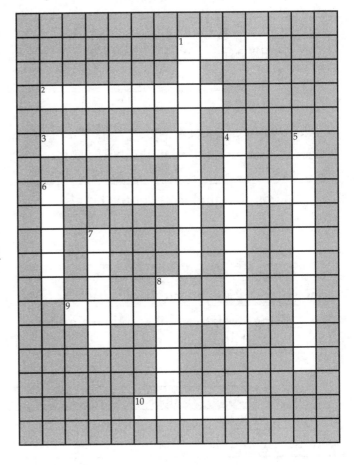

The Chemistry of Collagen

Chapter 20

Activity B

Name _____

Date _____ Period_____

Extracting collagen from bones is an essential step in making full-bodied stock. Place a check (✓) next to the best choice in each step below.

Step 1. To produce a full-bodied beef stock, you should use bones from animals with the highest collagen levels. Which of the bones described will yield the highest levels of collagen?

_____ Bones from mature animals.	_____ Bones from young animals.

Step 2. Certain parts of animals have higher levels of collagen than others. Which parts of the animal will yield the most collagen for your beef stock?

_____ Joints and feet	_____ Ribs and leg bones

Step 3. Bones are simmered in liquid to create stock. Which choice of liquids will best brighten the stock's flavor and improve its clarity?

_____ Water only.	_____ Water and small amount of wine.

Step 4. For bones to supply the best flavor to the stock, the right amount of liquid must be used. How much liquid should be used to extract the best flavor when simmering bones for stock?

_____ Enough liquid to cover the bones halfway.	_____ Enough liquid to cover bones with one to two inches of liquid.

Step 5. Gelatin is a protein that is derived from collagen and gives stock mouthfeel. How long should bones be simmered to extract sufficient gelatin to produce a beef stock?

_____ Bring stock to a boil and then simmer for at least 10 hours.	_____ Bring stock to a boil and then simmer for 3 to 5 hours.

Step 6. After collagen turns into gelatin in your stock, what happens to it?

_____ The gelatin dissolves into the simmering liquid.	_____ The gelatin rises to the surface and needs to be skimmed off.

Reviewing Key Concepts

Chapter 20

Activity C

Name _____

Date _____Period_____

Part 1: Stock Ingredients and Attributes

Circle the clue in parentheses that best completes each of the following statements.

1. Nutritive ingredients of stock are (**meat and bones**) (**bones and water**) (**bones and gelatin**).

2. Meats add (**mouthfeel**) (**flavor**) (**body**) to stock, while bones add (**mouthfeel**) (**flavor**) (**body**).

3. Aromatic ingredients of stock include (**salt, spices, and herbs**) (**vegetables, salt, and herbs**) (**vegetables, herbs, and spices**).

4. The universal vegetable flavoring in stock is mirepoix, which is a (**specific combination of vegetables**) (**paste made of boiled down vegetables**) (**combination of mushrooms and tomatoes**).

5. Most stocks are flavored with three herbs (**bay leaf, rosemary, and sage**) (**thyme, bay leaf, and parsley**) (**rosemary, parsley, and thyme**).

6. The nutritive and aromatic ingredients of stock are typically simmered in water. Sometimes wine is added, which (**brightens the flavor, but clouds the stock**) (**adds acidity that brightens the stock's flavor and improves overall clarity**) (**cuts acidity, which clears the stock**).

7. All well made stocks share the following four attributes: (**body, spices, color, and lightness**) (**flavor, color, taste, and body**) (**color, clarity, flavor, and body**).

8. Vegetable stocks are not true stocks because they are (**not flavorful**) (**used only for vegetarian cuisine**) (**not made from bones**).

9. The difference between white and brown vegetable stock is that in white vegetable stock vegetables are first raw or (**baked**) (**panfried**) (**sautéed**), and in brown vegetable stock vegetables are first (**boiled**) (**browned**) (**sautéed**).

10. Vegetable stocks differ from meat-based stocks in one important way—(**they have less flavor**) (**they are more acidic**) (**they contain no gelatin**).

11. Vegetable stocks lack the (**mouthfeel**) (**flavor**) (**clarity**) of meat-based stocks.

Activity C *(Continued)*   **Name** _____

Part 2: Bouillons, Broths, Bases, and Stocks

Read each statement below. Circle the letter *T* if the statement is true. If the statement is false, circle *F* and write the corrected statement on the lines that follow.

T   F   12. One ingredient that is not added to stock is salt.

_____

_____

T   F   13. White stocks are made using poultry, fish, or beef.

_____

_____

T   F   14. Deglazing greatly improves the flavor and color of a stock.

_____

_____

T   F   15. Bouillons and broths are prepared using different preparation processes.

_____

_____

T   F   16. Bouillons and broths have a bone-to-meat ratio that is greater than that of stocks.

_____

_____

T   F   17. Bouillons and broths typically require a more limited use of vegetables.

_____

_____

T   F   18. Broths and bouillons are classically reserved for soup production.

_____

_____

(Continued)

Activity C *(Continued)*   **Name** _____

T   F   19. The process for making broths and bouillons is specifically different from the process for making stocks.

_____

_____

T   F   20. A base is a concentrated instant powder or paste that dissolves in hot water to make a stocklike liquid.

_____

_____

T   F   21. Bases are slightly more expensive than stocks made from scratch.

_____

_____

T   F   22. Most bases are limited in their use in sauce making because they contain salt.

_____

_____

T   F   23. Bases that list fat as their first ingredient tend to be the highest quality.

_____

_____

Sauces

Culinary Terminology

Chapter 21

Activity A

Name _____

Date _____ Period_____

Part 1

Match the following terms and identifying phrases.

_____ 1. A yolk and cream mixture that is used to thicken liquids.

_____ 2. When this happens to egg or milk mixtures, the liquid and solid portions separate from each other.

_____ 3. A slurry made with flour.

_____ 4. A thickening sauce made from puréed fruits or vegetables.

_____ 5. Thickened liquids that complement other foods.

_____ 6. A method of gradually warming the temperature of egg yolks before adding them to a hot sauce.

_____ 7. A hot emulsified sauce that combines egg yolks and warm clarified butter.

_____ 8. A shortened version of demi-glace sauce.

_____ 9. A sauce that is made from a mother sauce.

_____ 10. Is classically made by reducing espagnole sauce to proper nappé consistency.

A. coulis

B. curdle

C. demi-glace sauce

D. derivative sauce

E. hollandaise sauce

F. jus lié

G. liaison

H. sauce

I. tempering

J. whitewash

(Continued)

Activity A *(Continued)*   **Name** _____

Part 2

_____ 11. The consistency of a sauce when it is thick
enough to coat the back of a spoon.

_____ 12. A mixture of cold liquid and starch used to
thicken sauces.

_____ 13. In the French sauce system, each of the five
sauces from which other sauces are produced.

_____ 14. A mixture of equal parts flour and fat by
weight that is cooked to varying degrees of
doneness and used to thicken liquids.

_____ 15. Classic name for white sauce.

_____ 16. A small onion that is stuck with several whole
cloves pushed through a bay leaf.

_____ 17. Made by slowly reducing brown stock, a bit of
tomato product, and brown roux for hours.

_____ 18. A sauce that is made by thickening a white
stock with a blond roux.

A. béchamel sauce

B. espagnole sauce

C. mother sauce

D. nappé

E. onion piqué

F. roux

G. slurry

H. velouté sauce

Roux Ratios

Chapter 21

Activity B

Name _____

Date _____Period_____

Ratios describe the relationship between two or more numbers. Chefs use ratios when thickening sauces. For example, when using roux to thicken liquid into a sauce, the amount of roux to liquid can be expressed as a ratio. For the very lightest sauces, chefs use 8 ounces of roux for every 1 gallon (128 oz.) of liquid. This ratio is written 8 to 128. This ratio can also be written 8:128 or 8/128. (*Remember, the backslash in a fraction or ratio is the same as saying "divide by."*)

But what if you only need to thicken 32 ounces of liquid? How would you calculate how much roux you need to make a light sauce? Start by calculating how much roux is needed per one ounce of liquid. You know that to make a light sauce you need

8 oz. roux per 128 oz. liquid

This can be written as a ratio

$$\frac{8}{128}$$

The ratio can be written as a division problem

$$8 \text{ oz. roux} \div 128 \text{ oz. liquid} = \frac{0.0625 \text{ oz. roux}}{\text{oz. liquid}}$$

Now you can calculate how much roux the chef needs to thicken 32 ounces of liquid to light consistency. If you know how much roux is needed per ounce of liquid, you simply multiply the ounces of liquid by that amount

$$\frac{0.0625 \text{ oz. roux}}{\text{oz. liquid}} \text{ x } 32 \text{ oz. liquid} = 2 \text{ oz. roux}$$

1. **A medium sauce recipe calls for 1 gallon of liquid thickened with 12 ounces of roux. Answer the following questions about the roux ratio for this preparation.**

   What is the ratio of roux to liquid?_____

   How much roux is needed to thicken one ounce of liquid to a medium sauce consistency? _____

   Calculate how much roux is needed to thicken 96 ounces of liquid to medium sauce consistency._____

(Continued)

Activity B *(Continued)*   **Name** _____

2. **A thick sauce recipe calls for 1 gallon of liquid thickened with 20 ounces of roux. Answer the following questions about the roux ratio for this preparation.**

    What is the ratio of roux to liquid?_____

    How much roux is needed to thicken one ounce of liquid to a thick sauce consistency?

    _____

    Calculate how much roux is needed to thicken 48 ounces of liquid to thick sauce consistency.

    _____

Reviewing Key Concepts

Chapter 21

Activity C

Name _____

Date _____Period_____

Part 1: The Five Roles of Sauces

Circle the clue in parentheses that best completes each of the following statements.

1. Two elements that sauces add, which improve the appearance of food are (**color and liquidness**) (**color and shine**) (**color and milkiness**).

2. (**Visual appeal**) (**Olfactory appeal**) (**Texture appeal**) is an element that sauces can add to a simple center of a plate item that allows the dish to command a higher value on the menu.

3. Sauces add richness to food especially sauces that are high in (**jus lié**) (**nappé**) (**fat**).

4. Sauces contribute flavors that (**disguise**) (**reduce**) (**complement**) or accent the flavors of a particular dish.

5. Sauces add (**texture**) (**moisture**) (**body**) to keep the dish from tasting dry and unappetizing.

Part 2: Thickening Agents

Match the following terms and identifying phrases.

_____ 6. Thickens liquids very quickly, but if liquid is not stirred as it is added, lumps may form.

_____ 7. This agent thickens by adding finely ground fruits, vegetables, seeds, or nuts.

_____ 8. This method requires egg yolk, mustard, or natural emulsifiers to hold it together.

_____ 9. This thickening agent is often mixed with a small amount of cream and must be added to the sauce gradually or curdling may result.

_____ 10. The three types of this thickener are all made from the same proportions of fat and flour.

_____ 11. Can be used to thicken sauces at the last minute, but can produce a flavor of raw flour.

_____ 12. Rarely used method today because it produces a somewhat pasty texture.

_____ 13. This method concentrates flavor as well as thickens liquid.

A. beurre manié

B. bread

C. egg yolk

D. emulsion

E. purée

F. reduction

G. roux

H. slurry

(Continued)

Activity C *(Continued)*   **Name** _____

Part 3: Classic System of Mother and Derivative Sauces

Use terms from the list to complete the chart that follows.

Allemande sauce	Cheddar sauce	White sauce
Béarnaise sauce	Fresh herbs sauce	White stock
Bordelaise sauce	Hollandaise sauce	
Brown stock	Tomato sauce	

Classical French Sauce System		
Mother Sauce	**Key Ingredient(s)**	**Derivative Sauces**
I. Brown sauce	A.	1. 2. Robert sauce
II.	A. Egg yolks B. Clarified butter	1. 2. Chantilly sauce
III.	A. Tomatoes B. Flavoring agents such as herbs	1. Paprika and cream sauce 2.
IV. Velouté sauce	A. B. Blond roux	1. 2. Suprême sauce
V.	A. White roux B. Onion C. Bay leaf D. Nutmeg	1. 2. Crême sauce

Part 4: Nontraditional Sauces

Complete the following statements about nontraditional sauces.

14. Beurre blanc is the name of a sauce composed almost entirely of_____ .

15. Broken butter sauces are basically just _____. (two words)

16. Beurre noisette is the French name for browned butter finished with _____. (two words)

17. Chutneys are similar to relishes, but use different_____ .

18. Salsas tend to be spicy hot due to the _____ from which they are made.

Soups

Culinary Terminology

Chapter 22

Activity A

Name _____

Date _____ Period _____

Circle the clue in parentheses that best completes each of the following statements.

1. The coagulated mixture of ground meat, vegetables, and egg whites that floats on top of stock during the clarifying process is called a **(raft)** **(bisque)** **(consommé)**.

2. **(Raft)** **(Clearmeat)** **(Chowder)** is an American seafood-based soup that is flavored with dairy product, bacon, and potato.

3. A mixture of ground meat, vegetables, and egg whites added to stock is called a **(raft)** **(clearmeat)** **(bisque)**.

4. **(Raft)** **(Clearmeat)** **(Bisque)** is seafood-based soup that is traditionally thickened with rice and flavored with sherry and brandy.

5. Due to the addition of cream and butter, **(purée)** **(cream)** **(bisque)** soups tend to be the richest and silkiest of soups.

6. **(Purée)** **(Cream)** **(Bisque)** soups are thickened using a purée of well-cooked ingredients.

7. A **(purée)** **(cream)** **(consommé)** soup is unique from other soups because it is made by clarifying stock.

8. Clearmeat that has been coagulated by albumin from egg white and is floating along with trapped impurities on top of stock is called a **(purée)** **(consommé)** **(raft)**.

9. **(Purée)** **(Clearmeat)** **(Consommé)** is a perfectly transparent and intensely flavored soup.

10. Often considered a luxury, **(purée)** **(cream)** **(bisque)** soup is often flavored with sherry, tinted red with tomato product, and fortified with cream.

11. Starchy foods such as legumes, potatoes, winter squashes, or rice are often the ingredients of a **(purée)** **(consommé)** **(bisque)** soup.

12. **(Purée)** **(Chowder)** **(Cream)** soups tend to be filling soups that were traditionally made and consumed by fishermen.

13. A soup that consists of milk or stock, thickened with both flour and puréed ingredients, and often finished with cream is a **(purée)** **(clearmeat)** **(cream)** soup.

Comparing Soup Categories

Chapter 22   Name _____

Activity B   Date _____Period_____

Read each statement below. Circle the letter *T* if the statement is true. If the statement is false, circle *F* and write the corrected statement on the lines that follow.

T   F   1.   Clear soups are divided into purée soups, cream soups, and bisques and chowders.

_____

_____

T   F   2.   Broth soup is unique from other soups because it is made by clarifying stock.

_____

_____

T   F   3.   Thick soups have a round mouthfeel because they are thickened.

_____

_____

T   F   4.   Minestrone, vegetable, and chicken noodle soups are examples of bisque soups.

_____

_____

T   F   5.   When consommé is finished cooking, it must be ladled out of the pot because pouring could break the raft and ruin the consommé.

_____

_____

T   F   6.   After cooking, broth soup should be strained through a coffee filter or cheesecloth.

_____

_____

T   F   7.   Cream soups are made from thickened milk, never from stock.

_____

_____

(Continued)

Activity B *(Continued)*   Name _____

T   F   8.   Purée soups get their thickening power from the starchy ingredients in the soup.

_____

_____

T   F   9.   Clear soups are thin, generally transparent, and have no vegetables or meat in them.

_____

_____

T   F   10.   Clear soups are divided into broth soups and consommés.

_____

_____

Reviewing Key Concepts

Chapter 22

Activity C

Name _____

Date _____ Period_____

Part 1: Specialty Soups

Circle the clue in parentheses that best completes each of the following statements.

1. Soups classically grouped under the heading of specialty soups are
(**traditional soups to which chefs have added a personal touch**)
(**soups that fall outside the description of traditional soup categories**).

2. A beet and red cabbage soup is a popular specialty cold soup called (**vichyssoise**)
(**borscht**) (**gazpacho**).

3. A cold cream of potato leek soup is a popular specialty cold soup called (**vichyssoise**)
(**borscht**) (**gazpacho**).

4. A Spanish soup of puréed tomatoes, red peppers, garlic, and cucumber is a popular
specialty cold soup called (**vichyssoise**) (**borscht**) (**gazpacho**).

Part 2: The Role of Soup Garnishes

Complete the following statements in the space provided.

5. Adding a garnish to a finished soup adds visual appearance, texture, and _____

    _____ .

6. Garnishes should be bite-size pieces or smaller because _____

    _____ .

7. Garnishes should be tender because _____

    _____ .

8. Fatty or oily garnishes should be avoided for consommés because _____

    _____ .

9. Garnishes should complement the soup in style and _____ .

10. The guideline for temperature of soup garnishes is that garnishes for hot soups
should be served _____ and garnishes for cold soups should be
served _____ .

Activity C *(Continued)*   **Name** _____

Part 3: Serving Soups

Circle the clue in parentheses that best completes each of the following statements.

11. To serve a successful hot soup, the temperature of the soup must be (**boiling**) (**slightly warmer than lukewarm**) (**very hot**).

12. To serve a successful cold soup, the temperature of the soup must be (**cool**) (**slightly cooler than room temperature**) (**very cold**).

13. When serving soup, the serving container should be (**the same temperature as the soup**) (**lukewarm for both hot and cold soups**) (**slightly chilled for both hot and cold soups**).

14. An advantage of using a soup plate rather than a soup bowl is that (**soup plates keep hot soup hotter and cold soup cooler**) (**soup plates make a beautiful presentation**).

15. An advantage of using a soup bowl rather than a soup plate is that (**bowls offer a more traditional appearance**) (**soup tends to slosh out or onto the sides of the plate**).

16. Soup should always be served (**in front of the customer**) (**as soon as it is portioned**).

Notes

Vegetable Identification

Identifying Common Fresh Vegetables

Chapter 23

Activity A

Name _____

Date _____Period_____

Part 1

First, complete any partial terms. Place a word in each space to complete the name of the vegetable. Next, place the letter of each vegetable in its correct category in the chart.

Categories of Vegetables		
Cabbages	Fruit Vegetables	Greens
Legumes	Mushrooms	Onions
Root Vegetables	Seeds	Squashes, Winter
Squashes, Summer	Squashes, Other	Stalks and Shoots

A. acorn _____

B. asparagus

C. beets

D. broccoli

E. butternut _____

F. cardoons

G. cauliflower

H. celery root

I. chile peppers

J. corn

K. eggplant

L. French beans

M. green beans

N. jicama

O. leeks

P. morels

Q. napa _____

R. parsnips

S. peas

T. pumpkins

U. red _____

V. savoy _____

W. shallots

X. spinach

Y. Swiss chard

Z. tomatoes

AA. turnips

BB. wax beans

CC. yellow _____

(Continued)

Activity A (*Continued*)   **Name** _____

Part 2

First, complete any partial terms. Place a word in each space to complete the name of the vegetable. Next, place the letter of each vegetable in its correct category in the chart.

Categories of Vegetables		
Cabbages	Fruit Vegetables	Greens
Legumes	Mushrooms	Onion
Root Vegetables	Seeds	Squashes, Winter
Squashes, Summer	Squashes, Other	Stalks and Shoots

A. artichokes

B. avocado

C. black-eyed peas

D. Brussels sprouts

E. button _____

F. carrots

G. celery

H. chayote

I. collard _____

J. cucumbers

K. fennel

L. garlic

M. green _____

N. kale

O. lentils

P. mustard _____

Q. okra

R. pattypan

S. portobello _____

T. radishes

U. red _____

V. scallions

W. shell beans

X. sweet peppers

Y. tomatilloes

Z. truffles

AA. turnip _____

BB. yellow _____

CC. zucchini

Selecting Vegetables

Chapter 23

Activity B

Name _____

Date _____ Period_____

Part 1: Recognizing Quality Factors in Vegetables

Read each statement below. Circle the letter *T* if the statement is true. If the statement is false, circle *F* and write the corrected statement on the lines that follow.

T   F   1.   Extra large cucumbers with a yellowish color are the best choice for cucumbers.

_____

_____

T   F   2.   Soft onions that are beginning to sprout are the best choice.

_____

_____

T   F   3.   Quality asparagus has tight tips, straight stalks, and no more than an inch of woody base at the bottom of the stalk.

_____

_____

T   F   4.   The best quality greens may have yellow spots.

_____

_____

T   F   5.   Choose cabbage that has enough space between leaves for the head to breathe.

_____

_____

T   F   6.   Carrots should not have green shoulders and should break with a snap when bent.

_____

_____

T   F   7.   Brussels sprouts should have firm compact heads and good green color.

_____

_____

(Continued)

Activity B (*Continued*)   **Name** _____

T F   8. The caps of button mushrooms should be white and the gills should be dark and open.

_____

_____

T F   9. Choose corn with small kernels, dry silk, and a green husk.

_____

_____

T F   10. Eggplant should have a firm texture and dull skin.

_____

_____

Part 2: Fresh Vegetables in Season

For each vegetable listed, circle the choice that best describes its availability or peak season. Some answers may include more than one season.

Vegetable	Season (circle all that apply)				
Root vegetables are at their peak during	spring	summer	fall	winter	year-round
Cabbages are available	spring	summer	fall	winter	year-round
Broccoli is available	spring	summer	fall	winter	year-round
Asparagus peaks	spring	summer	fall	winter	year-round
Fresh morel mushrooms are available	spring	summer	fall	winter	year-round
Wax beans are available	spring	summer	fall	winter	year-round
Cauliflower is available	spring	summer	fall	winter	year-round
Zucchini is fresh	spring	summer	fall	winter	year-round
Cardoons are ready	spring	summer	fall	winter	year-round
Pattypan is fresh	spring	summer	fall	winter	year-round
Green beans are available	spring	summer	fall	winter	year-round
Italian beans are available	spring	summer	fall	winter	year-round
Fresh chanterelle mushrooms are available	spring	summer	fall	winter	year-round
Truffles are harvested in	spring	summer	fall	winter	year-round
French beans are available	spring	summer	fall	winter	year-round

Reviewing Key Concepts

Chapter 23

Activity C

Name _____

Date _____ Period _____

Part 1: Purchase Forms of Vegetables

Describe the common purchase forms of packaging for the following fresh vegetables. There may be more than one form of packaging.

1. Dry onions: _____

   _____

2. Beets without tops: _____

   _____

3. Bunch spinach: _____

   _____

4. Asparagus: _____

   _____

5. Standard cucumbers: _____

   _____

6. Regular tomatoes: _____

   _____

7. French beans: _____

   _____

8. Button mushrooms: _____

   _____

Activity C (*Continued*)   **Name** _____

Part 2: Processing and Grading Vegetables

Circle the clue in parentheses that best completes each of the following statements.

9. Processed vegetables include **(only canned vegetables) (only frozen vegetables) (both canned and frozen vegetables)**.

10. Canned vegetables are **(more) (less)** consistent in quality and yield than fresh vegetables.

11. Green vegetables are more likely to lose their color when **(canned) (frozen)**.

12. Canned vegetables are **(more) (less)** expensive than fresh vegetables.

13. Canned vegetables often have a slightly different flavor and appearance than their fresh counterparts because they are **(inferior quality) (cooked during the canning process)**.

14. Frozen vegetables are **(less) (more)** expensive than canned vegetables.

15. Cooking time for frozen vegetables is often **(more) (less)** than for fresh vegetables.

16. The USDA has a **(mandatory) (voluntary)** grading system for both fresh and processed vegetables.

17. For most fresh vegetables, the top grade is either No. 1 or **(Extra Standard) (Fancy)**.

18. For canned or frozen vegetables, the grades are US Grade A or **(Extra Standard) (Standard) (Fancy)**; US Grade B or **(Extra Standard) (Fancy) (Standard)**; US Grade C or **(Standard) (Fancy) (Extra Standard)**.

19. When grading processed vegetables, the product is scored on its character, color, **(firmness) (attractiveness) (uniformity of size)**, and absence of defects.

20. Heat in chile peppers is measured in **(ancho) (Scoville heat units) (capsaicin)**.

Vegetable Cookery

Culinary Terminology

Chapter 24

Activity A

Name _____

Date _____ Period _____

Circle the clue in parentheses that best completes each of the following statements.

1. The process of plunging vegetables into ice water after cooking is called (**blanching**) (**glazing**) (**shocking**).

2. (**Cellulose**) (**Al dente**) (**Blanching**) literally means "to the tooth." This term is used to describe food that is cooked to the point that it (**gives some slight resistance to the tooth**) (**requires no actual chewing**).

3. In cooking, the process of giving something a shiny coating is called (**blanching**) (**glazing**) (**shocking**).

4. The rigid tissue of plants is composed mainly of microscopic fibers called (**cellulose**) (**al dente**) (**chlorophyll**).

5. The purpose of shocking is to (**preserve color**) (**stop the cooking process**) (**allow vegetables to absorb liquid**).

6. The process of partially cooking an item in rapidly boiling water is called (**blanching**) (**glazing**) (**shocking**).

7. Vegetables cooked al dente are (**crunchy**) (**mushy**) (**neither mushy nor crunchy**).

8. The human digestive system is unable to break down (**cellulose**) (**al dente**) (**chlorophyll**).

9. The chemical that gives green vegetables their color is (**cellulose**) (**al dente**) (**chlorophyll**).

10. Chefs use a sauce, reduced stock, or a process similar to sautéing for (**blanching**) (**glazing**) (**shocking**) vegetables.

11. In addition to seasoning vegetables, adding salt during cooking also helps preserve the (**cellulose**) (**al dente**) (**chlorophyll**) in the vegetables.

How Does Cooking Affect Vegetables?

Chapter 24

Activity B

Name _____

Date _____Period_____

Read each statement below. Circle the letter *T* if the statement is true. If the statement is false, circle *F* and write the corrected statement on the lines that follow.

T   F   1.   Cooking breaks down cellulose in vegetables, making the texture more appealing and easier to digest.

_____

_____

T   F   2.   The pH of the liquid used to cook vegetables affects their color. The pigments of yellow-orange vegetables are most affected.

_____

_____

T   F   3.   Cooking affects the texture of vegetables. Established cooking times are not always reliable so chefs test vegetables at the thinnest part to see if they are properly cooked.

_____

_____

T   F   4.   The colors of red, white, and green vegetables are enhanced by being cooked in an acidic solution.

_____

_____

_____

T   F   5.   Nutrients in vegetables can become dissolved in cooking water.

_____

_____

(Continued)

Activity B (*Continued*)   **Name** _____

T   F   6.   A slightly alkaline solution preserves the color in red and white vegetables.

_____

_____

T   F   7.   Chefs try to limit the time vegetables are exposed to air, light, and heat in order to retain nutrients as much as possible.

_____

_____

T   F   8.   To achieve proper texture, chefs determine cooking method and length of cooking time based on the amount of chlorophyll in vegetables.

_____

_____

T   F   9.   Adding baking soda to cooking water for green vegetables helps preserve their green color as well as their texture and nutrients.

_____

_____

T   F   10.   Cooking preserves the properties of natural sugars in vegetables and keeps them from caramelizing.

_____

_____

Cooking Vegetables

Chapter 24

Activity C

Name _____

Date _____ Period_____

Part 1: Parcooking

Circle the clue in parentheses that best completes each of the following statements.

1. Parcooking vegetables saves time during busy service periods, allows vegetables to be finished a variety of ways, allows vegetables with different textures and colors to be properly cooked when served together, and gives better control **(of nutrients)** **(over the cooking process)** **(of flavors)**.

2. Blanching is done as quickly as possible to preserve **(texture and color)** **(color and nutrients)** **(texture, color, and nutrients)**.

3. To blanch vegetables properly, add them to water that is **(cool)** **(almost simmering)** **(rapidly boiling)**.

4. Once vegetables are blanched to correct doneness, you should stop the cooking process by shocking which involves **(turning off heat and setting pan aside)** **(plunging vegetables into ice water and letting them sit)** **(plunging vegetables into ice water and immediately draining them)**.

Part 2: Finishing Techniques

On the space provided before each of the statements below, write *sautéing, glazing,* or *gratiner* to indicate the type of finishing method being described.

_____ 5. Vegetables are tossed with butter and a sweet syrupy ingredient that adds both flavor and a glossy shine.

_____ 6. Vegetables are placed in a sauteuse and quickly tossed over moderate heat with whole butter, salt, and pepper.

_____ 7. This technique works best with vegetables that are complemented by a sweet flavoring, such as root vegetables.

_____ 8. Béchamel-based sauces, cheese, or bread crumbs are often used to create a browned surface on vegetable dishes under a broiler or salamander; or in a hot oven.

_____ 9. Vegetables are finished with a sauce or reduced stock.

(Continued)

Activity C *(continued)*   **Name** _____

Part 3: Cooking Methods

Circle the clue in parentheses that best completes each of the following statements.

10. Moist-heat cooking methods include (**steaming, stir-frying, and stewing**) (**steaming, stewing, and braising**) (**steaming, grilling, and stewing**).

11. Dry-heat cooking methods include (**stir-frying, deep frying, baking, roasting, braising, and grilling**) (**stir-frying, deep frying, baking, roasting, stewing, and grilling**) (**stir-frying, deep frying, baking, roasting, and grilling**).

12. Vegetables to be (**roasted**) (**deep-fried**) (**stir-fried**) should be cut in small, even pieces for proper cooking.

13. Vegetables are (**steamed**) (**stewed**) (**braised**) by partially covering them with a flavored liquid and then simmering.

14. Vegetables to be (**grilled**) (**braised**) (**deep-fried**) should be cut thick enough so they do not dry out and large enough so they don't fall through the rack.

15. (**Baking and roasting**) (**Stewing and baking**) (**Steaming and stir-frying**) are often done with whole vegetables.

16. Because delicate vegetables such as spinach or pea pods are easy to overcook, (**stir-frying**) (**braising**) (**steaming**) is not a recommended cooking method for these vegetables.

17. Vegetables to be (**roasted**) (**deep-fried**) (**stir-fried**) are coated with a breading or batter before cooking to seal in moisture and keep them from becoming too greasy.

18. Vegetables are braised (**in the oven**) (**on the stove top**) (**on the stove top or in the oven**).

19. The main difference between the stewing and braising processes is the (**vegetables are cut smaller**) (**cooking temperature is higher**) (**lid is kept tighter**) in the stewing process.

Starch Identification

Culinary Terminology

Match the following terms and identifying phrases.

_____ 1. Any rice sold with the bran layer left attached.

_____ 2. Not a variety of potato but an immature potato of any variety.

_____ 3. A rice that has been fully cooked and then freeze-dried.

_____ 4. The first part of the grain kernel that lies just under the husk and is rich in fiber.

_____ 5. Rice in which the bran layer has been pearled during the milling process.

_____ 6. Type of potato that is high in starch and typically used for baked potatoes.

_____ 7. Rice that has been parboiled to remove surface starch.

_____ 8. A hard variety of wheat that is a favored pasta ingredient.

_____ 9. The smallest part of the grain kernel and a source of fat.

_____ 10. The largest part of the grain kernel.

_____ 11. Potato that is relatively low in starch and typically used when boiling potatoes.

_____ 12. The enlarged part of the underground root of potato plants that is eaten.

A. bran

B. brown rice

C. converted rice

D. endosperm

E. germ

F. instant rice

G. mealy potato

H. new potato

I. semolina

J. tuber

K. waxy potato

L. white rice

Choosing the Right Potato

Chapter 25

Activity B

Name _____

Date _____ Period_____

Complete the chart below by writing *mealy, all-purpose, specialty,* or *waxy* to indicate the type of potato each variety is. Answer the questions that follow.

Potato Varieties and Type	
Variety	**Type**
Fingerling	
Long White	
Peruvian Blue	
Round Red	
Round White	
Russet Burbank	
Yukon Gold	

1. Which variety of potato is the best choice for baked potatoes?

   _____

2. Which variety of potato is the best choice for boiled potatoes?

   _____

3. Which variety of potato is the best choice for frying potatoes?

   _____

4. Which variety of the potato might be sold as a new potato?

   _____

   _____

5. Why are sweet potatoes and yams not included in the varieties list above?

   _____

Recognizing Common Grains and Grain Products

Chapter 25

Activity C

Name _____

Date _____Period_____

Part 1

Match the following terms and identifying phrases.

_____ 1. Coarsely ground hominy, commonly cooked as a hot cereal and often served with breakfast in the southern United States.

_____ 2. Finely milled flour made from hominy. Use to make the outside coating for tamales.

_____ 3. Noodles made from rice flour.

_____ 4. The only grain native to the America's.

_____ 5. A variety of wheat favored as a pasta ingredient because its texture allows pasta to stay firmer for longer.

_____ 6. The most important of the five grains that have fed Western civilization for the last 12,000 years.

_____ 7. Whole kernels of corn that has been treated with lye. Can be served as a side dish or an ingredient in soups and stews.

_____ 8. Primarily used as a flavoring in fermented beverages and bread products.

_____ 9. One of the oldest grains eaten by people. Today, most is used to make beer or animal feed, but a pearled version is used in soups and stews.

_____ 10. Not a true rice but the seed from a water plant that grows in the upper United States. Has a nutty flavor when cooked.

_____ 11. Fine pastalike product made from hard durum wheat. Can be steamed or cooked in a liquid and is traditionally served in North Africa with stews.

A. barley

B. corn

C. couscous

D. grits

E. hominy

F. masa harina

G. rice noodles

H. rye

I. semolina

J. wheat

K. wild rice

Activity C (*Continued*)   **Name** _____

Part 2

Match the following terms and identifying phrases.

_____ 1. Made by milling a special type of corn into different size grinds. Used for coating fried products, in breads, and as a cooked cereal called mush.

_____ 2. A medium-sized, round tube of pasta.

_____ 3. Also called *soba*, is popular in Japan. Used hot in soup or cold with a dipping sauce.

_____ 4. Most often cooked in liquid and eaten as hot oatmeal, but also added to breads.

_____ 5. Popular Asian noodle also called wheat noodles. Typically served in soups or fried crisp and served as a pancake or used to garnish.

_____ 6. Pasta shaped like a wagon wheel, often used in soups or pasta salad.

_____ 7. Long, thin, delicate pasta also called fidelini.

_____ 8. Long, twisted shaped pasta served with a sauce or broken and added to soup or salad.

_____ 9. Was a staple of the Chinese diet before rice. Typically boiled into porridge.

_____ 10. Noodles made from bean starch and prepared in ways similar to rice noodles.

_____ 11. Whole wheat kernels without the hull. Good source of dietary fiber.

_____ 12. Long, flat pasta that is typically used in casseroles.

_____ 13. The favorite pasta in the United States.

_____ 14. A finely milled corn flour used as a coating or a thickening agent for hot liquids.

_____ 15. A small tube pasta often used for baked dishes and pasta salads.

_____ 16. The seed of a grass plant grown in flooded fields called paddies.

_____ 17. Long, flat pasta about ¼ inch (1 cm) wide. It is served with a variety of sauces.

_____ 18. Made by removing the bran layer from wheat and then steaming and drying the product. Can be ground into different textures and soaked in water to be eaten raw or cooked.

_____ 19. Long pasta about 3/16 inch (0.5 cm) wide.

_____ 20. The Italian version of cornmeal. Used to prepare Italian side dish or entrée.

A. angel hair

B. bean starch noodles

C. buckwheat noodles

D. bulgur

E. cornmeal

F. cornstarch

G. egg noodles

H. fettucini

I. fusilli

J. lasagna

K. linguine

L. manicotti

M. millet

N. oats

O. polenta

P. rice

Q. rotelle

R. spaghetti

S. wheat berries

T. ziti

Starch Cookery

Culinary Terminology

Chapter 26

Activity A

Name _____

Date _____ Period _____

Circle the clue in parentheses that best completes each of the following statements.

1. The term *gaufrette* describes a (**tool for cutting potatoes into a waffle shape**) (**classification of deep-fried potatoes**) (**technique to increase the water content of potatoes before panfrying**).

2. If the recipe calls for cooking pasta al dente, you should continue cooking until the pasta is fully cooked (**and soft and mushy**) (**but not soft and mushy**) (**and crispy**).

3. To rehydrate a product, you must (**add water back to**) (**remove a quantity of water from**) the product.

4. A rice dish cooked at an active simmer while being stirred is (**risotto**) (**pilaf**).

5. A cooking method that includes sautéing the grain in hot fat, then adding hot liquid and simmering without stirring is (**risotto**) (**pilaf**).

6. (**Risotto**) (**Pilaf**) (**Al dente**) is a cooking method, as well as, the name of a traditional Italian rice dish.

7. A mandolin is typically used to prepare (**gaufrette**) (**al dente**) (**rehydrate**) potatoes.

8. Dry pasta requires a longer cooking time than fresh or fresh frozen pasta because cooking also acts to (**rehydrate**) (**al dente**) the pasta.

9. The (**boiling**) (**pilaf**) method is different from simmering because the aromatics are sweated and the grains of rice are coated with the fat before liquid is added.

10. "To the tooth" is a phrase used to describe pasta cooked (**al dente**) (**rehydrate**).

Calculating Rice to Liquid Ratio

Chapter 26

Activity B

Name _____

Date _____Period_____

Use the table below to answer the questions that follow. Write your answers in the spaces provided. Include the unit of measure in your answers. For metric answers, round up to the nearest whole number.

Rice to Liquid Ratios	
Rice Type	**Parts liquid to 1 part rice (by volume)**
Arborio	3
Basmati	1½ to 2
Brown, long grain	2½ to 3
Converted	1¾ to 2
White, long grain	1½ to 2
White, medium grain	1½ to 1¾
White, short grain	1½ to 1¾

Use the ratios in the table above to calculate an equal ratio consisting of different quantities. To calculate ratios when one of the quantities is unknown, you can find it by cross multiplying.

Example: You need to cook 4 cups of long grain brown rice. If you use the minimum amount of liquid, how much will you need? First, write the ratio for minimum liquid to long grain brown rice from the table above.

$$2½:1$$

Convert the fraction to a decimal for ease of use and write the ratio in the form of a division problem.

$$\frac{2.5 \text{ cups liquid}}{1 \text{ cup rice}}$$

Set up the problem to solve for the unknown (*n*) cups of liquid (in this case the "parts" are measured in cups).

$$\frac{2.5}{1} = \frac{n}{4}$$

Activity B *(Continued)*   **Name** _____

Use cross multiplication to solve for the unknown amount of liquid or rice.

$$\frac{2.5}{1} \diagdown \frac{n}{4}$$

1 x *n* = 2.5 x 4

***n* = 10 cups liquid**

Check your work by substituting your solution for the unknown *n*.

$$\frac{2.5}{1} \diagdown \frac{10}{4}$$

2.5 x 4 = 1 x 10

10 = 10

1. How much liquid do you need to cook 1 cup of arborio rice?_____

2. How much liquid do you need to cook 250 mL of converted rice?

3. What is the amount of arborio rice you can cook in 8 cups of liquid?

4. What is the minimum amount of liquid needed to cook 1 cup of white, medium grain rice?

_____

(Continued)

Activity B *(Continued)*   **Name** _____

5. What is the minimum amount of liquid needed to cook 500 mL of white, long grain rice?

6. What is the maximum amount of liquid needed to cook 500 mL of white, long grain rice?

7. Which two types of rice require the greatest liquid to grain ratio?

    _____ and _____

8. How much liquid do you need to cook 3 cups of arborio rice?

9. How much liquid do you need to cook ½ cup of arborio rice?

10. You have 2 cups of broth and want to use all of it as the liquid to cook a batch of rice. You have exactly 1 cup of each of the types of rice listed in the table. To use a proper grain to liquid ratio, which type(s) of rice could you choose to cook in your broth?

    _____

Reviewing Key Concepts

Chapter 26

Activity C

Name _____

Date _____ Period _____

Part 1: Cooking Potatoes

Complete each statement below by filling in the missing word or words.

1. The four most common methods for cooking potatoes are _____, _____, _____ and _____.

2. Potatoes are generally classified as being either _____ or _____.

3. The cooking methods that work best for _____ potatoes, commonly called baking potatoes, are _____ and _____.

4. The most common method of cooking _____ potatoes, commonly called boiling potatoes, is _____.

5. Bake potatoes in a _____ to _____ degree oven until done. You can test to see if a baking potato is done by _____.

6. Most deep-fried potatoes must be cooked in two stages. First, heat oil to _____°F (_____°C) and deep-fry for _____ to _____ minutes. Then heat oil to _____°F (_____°C) and deep-fry until golden brown and cooked internally.

Part 2: Cooking Grains

Match the following terms and identifying phrases.

_____ 7. Sauté grain in hot fat, then add hot liquid; simmer grain without stirring.

_____ 8. Keep rice at an active simmer while stirring; continually add hot seasoned liquid in small amounts until rice is tender.

_____ 9. Add the grain to a large amount of lightly salted boiling water.

_____ 10. Simmer a measured amount of grain in a measured amount of liquid in a covered pot for the appropriate time for the grain.

A. boiling

B. pilaf

C. risotto

D. simmering

(Continued)

Activity C *(Continued)*   **Name** _____

Part 3: Cooking Pasta

Summarize the four steps for cooking pasta in the space provided.

Step 1 _____

_____

Step 2 _____

_____

Step 3 _____

_____

Step 4 _____

_____

Culinary Terminology

Chapter 27

Activity A

Name _____

Date _____ Period _____

Match the following terms and identifying phrases.

_____ 1. When muscle tissue temporarily becomes extremely hard and stiff, shortly after the death of an animal.

_____ 2. A flexible but tough connective tissue found in ligaments and tendons, sometimes referred to as *silver skin*.

_____ 3. The time meat is allowed to rest after slaughter.

_____ 4. The internal organs and extremities that are removed before an animal or bird is butchered, also called *variety meats*.

_____ 5. Is strictly an assurance of safety and wholesomeness and not an indication of quality.

_____ 6. Classifying meat and poultry products according to quality.

_____ 7. A major division of the carcass.

_____ 8. The most prevalent connective tissue in meats.

_____ 9. Intramuscular fat.

_____ 10. The loss of water during the cooking process.

_____ 11. Protein that bundles muscle tissue together and connects muscle to bones, joints, and skin.

_____ 12. The offal meats commonly obtained from poultry.

A. aging

B. collagen

C. connective tissue

D. elastin

E. giblets

F. grading

G. inspection

H. marbling

I. offal

J. primal cut

K. rigor mortis

L. shrinkage

Reviewing Key Concepts

Chapter 27

Activity B

Name _____

Date _____ Period_____

Part 1: Meat Composition

On the space provided before each of the characteristics, write *muscle*, *connective tissue*, or *fat* to indicate the component of meat being described.

_____ 1. Is the most important factor in determining the toughness of a cut of meat.

_____ 2. Provides moisture, tenderness, and flavor to meats.

_____ 3. Is the most important part of meat.

_____ 4. Two types are subcutaneous and intramuscular.

_____ 5. Two types are elastin and collagen.

_____ 6. Cutting across the grain of this component creates a tender finished product.

Part 2: Aging

Circle the clue in parentheses that best completes each of the following statements.

7. While meat is in the (**rigor mortis**) (**dry aging**) (**wet aging**) stage, it is difficult to cut and extremely tough to eat.

8. The traditional method for aging meat is the (**rigor mortis**) (**dry aging**) (**wet aging**) process.

9. The process that ages meat while in vacuum-sealed plastic bags is the (**rigor mortis**) (**dry aging**) (**wet aging**) process.

10. (**Rigor mortis**) (**Dry aging**) (**Wet aging**) involves hanging meat in a low humidity refrigerator for as long as six weeks.

11. The (**rigor mortis**) (**dry aging**) (**wet aging**) process is a more cost effective aging method because there is reduced loss due to dry, moldy meat.

(Continued)

Activity B *(Continued)*   **Name** _____

Part 3: Selecting a Cooking Process

Read each statement below. Circle the letter *T* if the statement is true. If the statement is false, circle *F* and write the corrected statement on the lines that follow.

T   F   12. The most important consideration when trying to match the best cooking method for a cut of meat is the amount of fat in the meat.

_____

_____

T   F   13. Cuts of meat from the shoulder section of an animal are best simmered, braised, or stewed because these cuts are usually less tender.

_____

_____

T   F   14. Tender cuts are best cooked by moist methods.

_____

T   F   15. Cuts from along the back of an animal are best when simmered, braised, or stewed.

_____

_____

Part 4: Inspection and Grading

Circle the clue in parentheses that best completes each of the following statements.

16. **(Grading) (Inspection)** is an assurance of safety and wholesomeness and not an indication of quality.

17. **(Grading) (Inspection)** is classifying products according to quality.

18. **(Grading) (Inspection)** identifies the qualities that affect the tenderness and flavor of meat and poultry.

19. **(Grading) (Inspection)** is mandatory.

20. **(Grading) (Inspection)** is voluntary.

21. **(Grading) (Inspection)** is performed on live animals before slaughter and includes examination of animals' organs after slaughter.

22. **(Grading) (Inspection)** of meats is based on marbling, maturity, and muscle conformation.

23. **(Grading) (Inspection)** of poultry is based on size, flesh quality, and visible defects.

Foodservice Use of Meats and Poultry

Chapter 27

Activity C

Name _____

Date _____ **Period** _____

Part 1: Identifying

Read each statement below. Circle the letter *T* if the statement is true. If the statement is false, circle *F* and write the corrected statement on the lines that follow.

T   F   1.   There is just one way to cut subprimals regardless of their planned final use.

_____

_____

T   F   2.   Foodservice subprimals are essentially the same as retail cuts sold in supermarkets.

_____

_____

T   F   3.   The quality of meat is not affected by the way subprimals are cut and trimmed.

_____

_____

T   F   4.   IMPS numbers each identify a specific variation of cutting and trimming subprimals.

_____

_____

T   F   5.   Chefs typically specify meat items by name of cut when ordering from a purveyor.

_____

_____

Activity C *(Continued)*   **Name** _____

Part 2: Choosing Appropriate Cooking Methods for Meat

Complete the charts below with the primal cut and appropriate cooking method for each of the subprimal cuts of meat.

Beef and Veal		
Primal Cut	**Subprimal Cut**	**Appropriate Cooking Method**
Beef		
	Square Cut Chuck	
	Porterhouse Steak	
	Rib Eye Roll Steak, boneless	
Veal		
	Hotel Rack	
	Cutlets, boneless	

Lamb and Pork		
Primal Cut	**Subprimal Cut**	**Appropriate Cooking Method**
Lamb		
	Rack, frenched	
Pork		
	Tenderloin	

(Continued)

Activity C *(Continued)*   Name _____

Part 3: Choosing Appropriate Cooking Methods for Poultry

Complete the chart below by writing the appropriate cooking method for each poultry type and class.

Poultry		
Type	**Class**	**Appropriate Cooking Method**
Chicken		
	Cornish game hen	
	Broiler/fryer	
	Capon	
Turkey		
	Hen	
	Tom	
Duck		
	Duckling	
	Roaster	
Goose		
	Young	
	Mature	

Basic Meat and Poultry Preparation

Culinary Terminology

Name _____

Date _____ Period _____

Fill in each blank in the letter below with the appropriate culinary term from Chapter 28.

Dear Culinary Hopeful:

You asked about meat and poultry preparation in today's kitchen. Things have changed since the old days when every large food operation had a _____ on staff, who was responsible for all the cutting and trimming of meat items used in the operation. Today's professional kitchens rarely buy an entire animal carcass. However, there is still plenty of cutting and trimming to do. For example, in a process called _____, we cut meat or poultry into serving portions. We cut all of our _____, which is a portion-size piece cut from a large muscle or group of muscles. This portion may or may not have a bone; but a steak portion called a _____, always has a bone. Another variety, a thin, boneless steak that is prepared by cutting thin slices of a boneless muscle is called a

_____.

Another part of meat preparation is tying roasts. One of the reasons to tie a large roast is for _____ it, which simply means to cover it with a thin sheet of fat to keep it moist during cooking. Birds to be roasted whole are also tied. When referring to birds, tying is usually called _____. This process gives the cooked bird a pleasing appearance and ensures even cooking. Roasting poultry is common, but perhaps the most popular cut of poultry is the boneless chicken breast. In fine dining establishments, we commonly present each lobe of the breast with the first joint of the wing still attached. We call this cut

_____.

So as you can see, there are still plenty of opportunities for meat preparation in the contemporary professional kitchen.

Master Chef

Reviewing Key Concepts

Chapter 28

Name _____

Activity B

Date _____ Period_____

Part 1: Proper Handling and Storage

Circle the clue in parentheses that best completes each of the following statements.

1. Fresh meat and poultry should be stored (**below 30°F to 35°F [-1°C to 2°C])** (**at 30°F to 35°F [-1°C to 2°C])** (**above 30°F to 35°F [-1°C to 2°C]**).

2. Film-wrapped, vacuum-packed meats have a refrigerated shelf life of (**several days**) (**several weeks**) (**several months**) when kept in their sealed bags.

3. Meat and poultry should be stored on a tray or sheet pan to keep them (**from dripping on other items**) (**organized for quick location**) (**from warming**).

4. Never store raw meats or poultry (**below**) (**on the same level as**) (**above**) cooked or ready-to-eat items.

5. Sanitize (**major**) (**non-refrigerated**) (**all**) food-contact surfaces when storing meats and poultry.

Part 2: Poultry Fabrication

Circle the clue in parentheses that best completes each of the following statements.

6. To begin to split poultry in half, place the bird on the cutting board with the (**breast**) (**back**) toward you and the tail up. After splitting in half, the bird's backbone (**remains with one portion**) (**is cut away and removed**).

7. To cut poultry halves into quarters, you need to find the natural separation between the (**leg and wing**) (**breast and thigh**) (**leg and thigh**) and cut along that line.

8. Another term for preparing eight-cut portions of poultry is (**double quarter**) (**disjointed**).

9. To eight-cut a bird after quartering, the cut to make on the leg-and-thigh quarter is through the joint connecting the (**thigh and drumstick**) (**thigh and wing**) (**leg and wing**).

10. To eight-cut a bird after quartering, the cut to make on the breast-and-wing quarter is through the joint at the base of the (**breast**) (**leg**) (**wing**).

Reviewing Key Concepts

Chapter 28

Activity C

Name _____

Date _____ Period_____

Part 1: Common Meat Portions

Circle the clue in parentheses that best completes each of the following statements.

1. A **(steak) (chop) (cutlet) (roast)** is a portion-size piece of meat that is cut from a larger muscle or group of muscles.

2. Both a **(steak) (chop) (cutlet) (roast)** and a **(steak) (chop) (cutlet) (roast)** are types of **(steak) (chop) (cutlet) (roast)**.

3. A **(steak) (chop) (cutlet) (roast)** always has a bone.

4. A **(steak) (chop) (cutlet) (roast)** sometimes has a bone.

5. A **(steak) (chop) (cutlet) (roast)** never has a bone.

6. A **(steak) (chop) (cutlet) (roast)** is not a portion-size piece of meat.

Part 2: Portioning

Read each statement below. Circle the letter *T* if the statement is true. If the statement is false, circle *F* and write the corrected statement on the lines that follow.

T   F   7.   Uniformity in portions in the commercial kitchen is measured by appearance.

_____

_____

T   F   8.   Consistency in portion size is essential to customer satisfaction and product cost.

_____

_____

T   F   9.   Small inconsistencies in meat portions are not important but large ones can raise cost.

_____

_____

(Continued)

Activity C (*Continued*)   **Name** _____

T   F   10. Most chefs consider portion size variance of more than two ounces (60 g) unacceptable.

_____

_____

T   F   11. Many kitchens buy portion-cut meat and poultry rather than deal with cutting portioning themselves.

_____

_____

Dry-Heat Cooking Methods for Meat and Poultry

29

Culinary Terminology

Chapter 29

Activity A

Name _____

Date _____ Period _____

Match the following terms and identifying phrases. Some terms may be used more than once.

_____ 1. The process of coating foods with flour.

_____ 2. The process of browning meat to form an even crust.

_____ 3. The process that involves simmering pan drippings and liquid to dissolve the drippings.

_____ 4. When seasoning is added to flour used in this process, the product can be both coated and seasoned in one step.

_____ 5. The amount of cooking that continues after a large roast is removed from the oven.

_____ 6. This process does not work properly if the sauté pan is overloaded.

_____ 7. This process is the first step toward creating a sauce from the pan drippings of a sautéed item.

_____ 8. The deglazed drippings of a roast that are strained and seasoned.

_____ 9. Because of this effect, large roasts must be removed in advance of the final desired temperature being reached.

_____ 10. Thickened jus.

_____ 11. The French term for *juice*.

_____ 12. The thickening agent for this product may be roux or a slurry.

A. carryover cooking

B. deglazing

C. dredging

D. gravy

E. jus

F. searing

Comparing Approaches for Roasting

Chapter 29

Activity B

Name _____

Date _____ Period _____

Complete the concept chart below that compares the two approaches for roasting meats and poultry. Fill in each numbered shape with a phrase from the following list.

At a lower temperature.

Constant heat.

Creates a moist product.

In an oven at one temperature throughout.

More natural juices are lost.

On a range top.

Product might not brown.

Useful for products that won't brown in a short time.

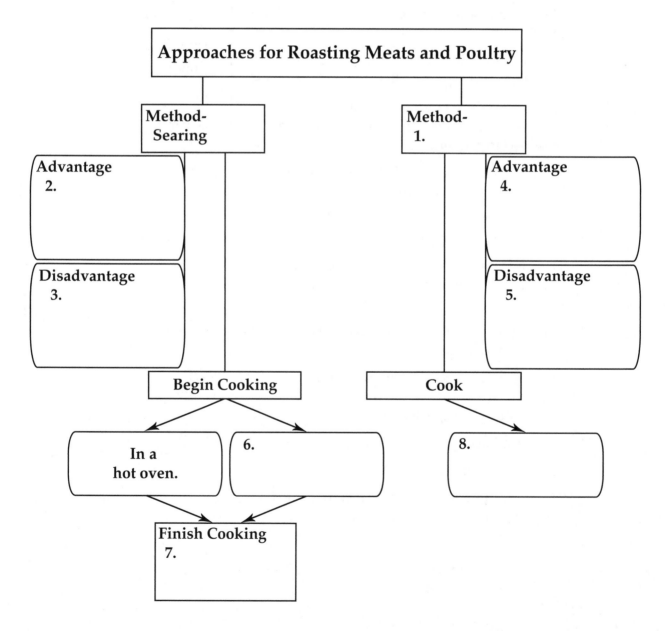

Reviewing Key Concepts

Chapter 29

Activity C

Name _____

Date _____ Period_____

Part 1: Sautéing and Pan Sauce Preparation

Read each statement below. Circle the letter *T* if the statement is true. If the statement is false, circle *F* and write the corrected statement on the lines that follow.

T   F   1.   Sautéing meat is a quick cooking process done over low heat.

_____

_____

T   F   2.   To sauté, the fat and product are added to the cold pan.

_____

_____

T   F   3.   A properly sautéed item is evenly seared.

_____

_____

T   F   4.   Any fat is suitable for sautéing.

_____

_____

T   F   5.   To create a sauce from the drippings left in the sauté pan, the meat must be removed from the pan and liquid must be added.

_____

_____

T   F   6.   The liquid used for deglazing is always water.

_____

_____

(Continued)

Activity C (*Continued*)   **Name** _____

T   F   7.   Sautéing is a good choice for large slices of tougher cuts of meat.

_____

_____

T   F   8.   When sautéing, fat should be about ¼ inch deep in pan.

_____

_____

Part 2: Grilling and Broiling

Circle the clue in parentheses that best completes each of the following statements.

9.   When (**broiling**) (**grilling**), the heat source is over the meat.

10.   When (**broiling**) (**grilling**), the heat source is under the meat.

11.   During grilling, drippings create smoke, which (**adds to**) (**has no affect on**) (**detracts from**) the flavor of the meat being cooked.

12.   Drippings from (**both broiling and grilling**) (**broiling**) (**grilling**) (**neither broiling nor grilling**) can be used to create sauces.

13.   Both the grilling and broiling processes should begin with a (**cold**) (**preheated**) grill or broiler.

14.   A clean grill is (**not essential**) (**very important**) to keep food from sticking during grilling.

15.   Meat or poultry (**should**) (**should not**) be brushed with oil or butter before grilling or broiling begins.

16.   A (**sharp fork**) (**tongs**) should be used to turn or move meat on the grill.

17.   Once the meat on a grill starts to sear, rotate it (**30 degrees**) (**45 degrees**) (**90 degrees**) to create cross markings.

18.   When broiling thicker pieces of meat or poultry, once the meat is seared it should be finished at a (**higher**) (**constant**) (**lower**) temperature.

19.   Testing for doneness by piercing the seared crust of a grilled steak or chop is (**accepted**) (**good**) (**poor**) technique.

20.   When testing for doneness, meat that is (**firmer**) (**softer**) will be more well done.

Moist-Heat and Combination Cooking Methods for Meat and Poultry

30

Culinary Terminology

Chapter 30

Activity A

Name _____

Date _____Period_____

Match the following terms and identifying phrases. Some problems may have more than one correct answer. Some terms may be used more than once.

_____ 1. Means for determining doneness of larger cuts cooked by simmering or braising.

_____ 2. Method that applies simmering or braising to bite-size pieces of meat or poultry.

_____ 3. Employs the techniques of first searing then cooking in liquid.

_____ 4. One of its main benefits is the infusion of flavor to the product being cooked.

_____ 5. Cooks foods in liquids at temperatures between 185°F and 205°F (85°C–96°C).

_____ 6. Is a combination of dry-heat and moist-heat cooking methods.

_____ 7. Enough liquid to fully cover the ingredients is used in this method.

_____ 8. Cooks foods in liquids at relatively low temperatures between 160°F and 180°F (71°C–82°C).

_____ 9. Means that when a long-tined fork or skewer is inserted into a cut of cooked meat, the meat easily slides off the fork.

_____ 10. Cooking method that produces a rich broth.

A. braising

B. fork-tender

C. poaching

D. simmering

E. stewing

Reviewing Key Concepts

Chapter 30

Activity B

Name _____

Date _____ Period_____

Part 1: Poaching

Read each statement below. Circle the letter *T* if the statement is true. If the statement is false, circle *F* and write the corrected statement on the lines that follow.

T   F   1.   Poaching is very important in meat and poultry cookery, but has a limited role with fish.

_____

_____

T   F   2.   The main benefit of poaching is its tenderizing effect.

_____

_____

T   F   3.   Poaching of meat and poultry products is often limited to tender cuts of young poultry, such as the breast.

_____

_____

T   F   4.   Poaching is not a recommended cooking method for sausage.

_____

_____

T   F   5.   Court bouillon is water flavored with aromatic herbs and mirepoix.

_____

_____

T   F   6.   Stock and vinegar are equally common poaching liquids.

_____

_____

(Continued)

Activity B *(Continued)*   **Name** _____

Part 2: Simmering

Circle the clue in parentheses that best completes each of the following statements.

7. Meat and poultry should never be cooked at a boil because extended exposure to the higher temperature causes (**the meat to fall off the bone**) (**the liquid to evaporate**) (**their proteins to toughen**).

8. Simmering (**is the most effective way of breaking down**) (**has little effect on**) (**slows the breaking down of**) collagen.

9. Cuts from the (**forequarter**) (**hindquarter**) of animals and (**mature**) (**immature**) poultry are best cooked by simmering.

10. The means for checking for doneness of large cuts cooked by simmering or braising is called (**firmness**) (**fork-tender**).

Reviewing Key Concepts

Chapter 30

Activity C

Name _____

Date _____Period_____

Part 1: Braising

Read each statement below. Circle the letter *T* if the statement is true. If the statement is false, circle *F* and write the corrected statement on the lines that follow.

T   F   1.   Braising is a combination of stewing and poaching cooking methods.

_____

_____

T   F   2.   Braising is used for tough cuts of meat and poultry to make them tender.

_____

_____

T   F   3.   Simmering, unlike braising, begins with searing.

_____

_____

T   F   4.   Braised dishes are more easily simmered in the oven than on the stove top.

_____

_____

T   F   5.   When braising, enough liquid to completely cover the meat should be added.

_____

_____

T   F   6.   Braising in an uncovered pan allows the item to cook without scorching.

_____

_____

(Continued)

Activity C *(Continued)*   **Name** _____

Part 2: Stewing

Circle the clue in parentheses that best completes each of the following statements.

7. Stews made by braising technique are most often prepared with (**poultry**) (**red meats**).

8. Simmering and braising cooking methods are called *stewing* when (**the cooking time is much longer**) (**the food being cooked is in bite-sizes pieces**) (**a stewing pan is used**).

9. Aromatic vegetables are often added (**at the beginning**) (**near the end**) of the cooking time.

10. Stews become rich as a result of the (**shorter cooking process required**) (**blending of flavors of the many ingredients**).

Notes

Fish and Shellfish Identification

31

Culinary Crossword

Chapter 31

Activity A

Name _____

Date _____ Period_____

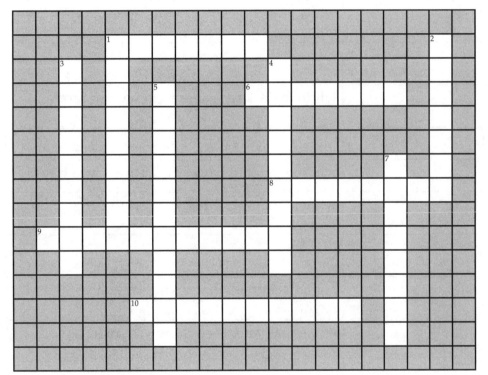

Across

1. Term that describes the process of separating the contents of a bivalve from its shell.
6. Family that consists of univalves, bivalves, and cephalopods.
8. Fish with two eyes on one side of their head and no eyes on the other side.
9. A category of mollusks known for its long arms that are covered with suckers, well-developed eyes, and sac that holds and ejects ink.
10. An aquatic species that has a hard and segmented exoskeleton, or shell.

Down

1. Water creatures that have no bones but their bodies are covered by hard external surfaces.
2. All species of fish that have an internal skeleton and swim in water.
3. Shellfish that have only one shell.
4. Fish with one eye on each side of their head and swim through the water with their dorsal fin upright. (two words)
5. The farming of fish and shellfish.
7. Shellfish that have two shells.

Recognizing Fresh Fish and Shellfish

Chapter 31

Activity B

Name _____

Date _____ Period_____

Part 1: Finfish

Complete the table below using information from the textbook.

Fish	Types	Characteristics of Flesh	Water–Fresh (F) Salt (S)
Marlin		white sometimes with pink, dense, meaty flesh	
Catfish			
		white to dark red, dense, chewy, moderate	S
Lake Trout			
		white, moderately toothy texture, mild flavor	
Snapper		white, moderately flaky, sweet flavor	
Cod			
		high oil content, firm textured flesh with mild flavor	F
Flounder		white, flaky textured flesh with mild flavor	
Pacific Salmon		pink, moderately flaky and oily, slightly strong flavor	
Grouper			
Trout	brook, rainbow		

(Continued)

Activity B *(Continued)*

Name _____

Part 2: Shellfish

For each of the following terms or phrases, place a check (✓) in the column for the type of shellfish being described.

	Crustacean	Mollusks		
		Bivalve	Univalve	Cephalopod
Crab				
Crayfish				
Hard-shell clams				
Has a hard, segmented shell, or exoskeleton				
Has long arms covered with suckers				
Has one shell				
Has two shells				
Maine lobster				
Mussels				
Octopus				
Oysters				
Rock (Spiny) lobster				
Scallops				
Shrimp				
Soft-shell clams				
Squid				

Judging the Quality of Fish and Shellfish

Chapter 31

Activity C

Name _____

Date _____ Period_____

Circle the clue in parentheses that best completes each of the following statements.

1. When judging the freshness of finfish, the gills should be a (**bright grey or brown**) (**bright rosy color**).

2. Fresh fish should have eyes that are (**flat and cloudy**) (**bulging and clear**) (**sunken and dry**).

3. Scales that (**are firmly attached to the skin**) (**come off easily when rubbed**) indicate a fish is fresh.

4. A fresh saltwater fish should smell (**strong and pungent**) (**oceanlike**) around the (**head and gills**) (**gut and head**) (**gills and gut**).

5. Fresh fish should feel (**firm but leave a distinct impression**) (**flabby but leave a slight impression**) (**firm and leave no impression**) when pressed.

6. Fresh cuts from saltwater fish should have a (**strong, salty smell**) (**pleasant oceanlike aroma**).

7. Boneless cuts from fresh fish should (**show no line**) (**show a clear line**) at the crease when the cut is gently folded and unfolded.

8. Both octopus and squid should have (**a distinct strong smell**) (**no particularly strong smell**).

9. Squid and octopus should be (**soft but firm**) (**hard and stiff**) (**firm and slightly elastic**).

10. Dark discoloration, especially on the body of the octopus or wings of the squid, is (**a warning sign the product may be old or has been mishandled**) (**totally normal and no indication of quality**).

Farming and Processing Fish

Chapter 31

Activity D

Name _____

Date _____ Period_____

Part 1: Processed Fish Products

Read each statement below. Circle the letter *T* if the statement is true. If the statement is false, circle *F* and write the corrected statement on the lines that follow.

T   F   1.   It is possible to thaw individual pieces of shrimp from block frozen shrimp.

_____

_____

T   F   2.   Traditionally, fish were preserved in salt because the large amount of salt drew moisture into the fish keeping it fresh and free from bacterial growth.

_____

_____

T   F   3.   Marinated herring is an example of seafood preserved in acidic liquid.

_____

_____

T   F   4.   Seafood to be salted is generally smoked first.

_____

_____

T   F   5.   Most smoked products do not need refrigeration.

_____

_____

T   F   6.   Canned products are raw, shelf stable, and often less expensive than the fresh equivalent.

_____

_____

(Continued)

Activity D *(Continued)*   **Name** _____

Part 2: Aquaculture

Read each statement below. Circle the letter *T* if the statement is true. If the statement is false, circle *F* and write the corrected statement on the lines that follow.

T   F   7.   Aquaculture takes place both in the wild or within man-made structures.

_____

_____

T   F   8.   Some of the most common aquaculture products include salmon, swordfish, and halibut.

_____

_____

T   F   9.   There is general agreement that aquaculture has a positive effect on the environment.

_____

_____

T   F   10.   Chefs, in general, find no difference between wild and aquaculture products.

_____

_____

T   F   11.   Foodservice is increasingly using aquaculture products.

_____

_____

Fish and Shellfish Preparation and Cookery

32

Identifying Basic Fabrication Forms of Fish

Chapter 32

Activity A

Name _____

Date _____ Period_____

Part 1

Match the following terms and identifying statements.

_____ 1. A totally edible product with no skin or bones.

_____ 2. A fish that has its head and collar removed and its tail and fins trimmed.

_____ 3. Fish that has been slit on the belly and its internal organs removed.

_____ 4. Crosscut individual portions that often include the backbone and skin.

_____ 5. The entire fish, as it was when it was caught.

_____ 6. The muscle that has been removed from the carcass of the fish.

_____ 7. Fish without the head, collar, or narrow tail section allowing for uniform steaks to be cut.

A. center cut

B. drawn

C. dressed

D. fillet

E. skinless fillets

F. steaks

G. whole

Part 2

Circle the clue in parentheses that best completes each of the following statements.

8. It is uncommon to buy (**center cut**) (**drawn**) (**whole**) fish.

9. Fish are sold drawn because this form (**allows oil to drain**) (**improves shelf life**).

10. A variety of the fillet fabrication form is (**butterfly**) (**round**) (**flat**).

11. The fabrication form (**center cut**) (**dressed**) (**whole**) is commonly done with trout and other small fish that will be panfried, baked, or grilled.

12. A variety of the fillet fabrication form is (**sûpremes**) (**gutted**) (**flat**).

Reviewing Key Concepts

Chapter 32

Name _____

Activity B

Date _____ Period _____

Part 1: Preparing Shellfish for Cooking

Read each statement below. Circle the letter *T* if the statement is true. If the statement is false, circle *F* and write the corrected statement on the lines that follow.

T   F   1.   Sometimes the last section of the shell and tail of shrimp may be left on for presentation.

_____

_____

T   F   2.   The dark vein along the back of shrimp enhances the taste of the product.

_____

_____

T   F   3.   Clams need to be debearded by pulling off the fibers that stick out of the shell.

_____

_____

T   F   4.   To open an oyster, hold the oyster on the work surface with the cupped part of the shell on top.

_____

_____

T   F   5.   Take care to leave the detached oyster whole and uncut.

_____

_____

(Continued)

Activity B *(Continued)*   **Name** _____

Part 2: Storing Fresh Finfish and Shellfish

Read each statement below. Circle the letter *T* if the statement is true. If the statement is false, circle *F* and write the corrected statement on the lines that follow.

T   F   6.   Fresh fish must be stored on crushed ice because most commercial refrigeration is not cold enough to store it safely.

_____

_____

T   F   7.   When stored on ice, a way must be found to keep the melting water on the fish.

_____

_____

T   F   8.   Mollusks should be stored at 40°F (4°C) to keep them alive.

_____

_____

T   F   9.   Cephalopods should be stored in the same manner as mollusks.

_____

_____

Dry- and Moist-Heat Cooking

Chapter 32

Activity C

Name _____

Date _____ Period _____

Part 1: Dry-Heat Methods

Circle the clue in parentheses that best completes each of the following statements.

1. Many chefs prefer (**clarified butter**) (**fish oil**) (**shortening**) for sautéing fish.

2. Browned butter is a classical preparation called (**beurre noisette**) (**court bouillon**) (**pin bones**).

3. Thick pieces of fish that are not completely cooked after sautéing, may be (**sliced and recooked**) (**deep fried**) (**finished in the oven**).

4. Fish is always dredged in (**clarified butter**) (**breading or batter**) (**salt**) before panfrying.

5. Fish should be deep-fried until the coating is (**light tan**) (**golden brown**) (**dark brown**).

6. The most important consideration for grilling fish is the (**size of the grill**) (**choice of fish**).

7. (**Firm-fleshed**) (**Soft-fleshed**) fish are best for grilling.

8. Broiling is an easy way to cook (**some firm-fleshed varieties of fish**) (**only delicate shellfish**) (**most any variety of fish or seafood**).

9. For delicately textured fish and seafood items, (**broiling**) (**baking**) lessens the chance of overcooking.

10. When grilling, more (**delicate**) (**firm**) items may be finished in the oven.

Part 2: Moist-Heat Methods

Circle the clue in parentheses that best completes each of the following statements.

11. Deep poaching is best for (**large, whole dressed**) (**small, filleted**) fish.

12. The preferred liquid for deep poaching is (**beurre noisette**) (**court bouillon**) (**pin bones**).

13. The poaching method that fully covers the item is (**deep**) (**shallow**) poaching.

14. The poaching method that partially covers the item is (**deep**) (**shallow**) poaching.

15. Steaming is a cooking method best used on (**tender fish**) (**firm fish**) (**shellfish**).

16. Fish, cooked by any method, should be cooked only long enough to allow the (**protein to fully coagulate**) (**juices to run clear**) (**skin to fully brown**).

Hot Sandwiches and Pizza

Hot Sandwiches and Their Ingredients

Chapter 33

Activity A

Name _____

Date _____ Period _____

Part 1

Read each statement below. Circle the letter *T* if the statement is true. If the statement is false, circle *F* and write the corrected statement on the lines that follow.

T   F   1.   There is little difference between hot and cold sandwiches other than part or all of a hot sandwich is served hot.

_____

_____

T   F   2.   Most hot sandwiches contain several hot fillings.

_____

_____

T   F   3.   Hot sandwiches can be divided into two categories—sandwiches made using hot fillings and those made using deep-fried ingredients.

_____

_____

T   F   4.   Hot sandwiches that mix hot and cold ingredients are best when temperatures are balanced and the whole sandwich is lukewarm.

_____

_____

T   F   5.   Hamburger must be cooked to a minimum of 155°F (68.3°C) to ensure that any *E. coli* in the meat is dead.

_____

_____

(Continued)

Activity A *(Continued)*   **Name** _____

T   F   6.   Sandwiches made from deep-fried ingredients are best prepared early and kept in a warmer.

_____

_____

T   F   7.   Whole cooked sandwiches differ from hot filling sandwiches in that the entire sandwich is cooked and served hot.

_____

_____

T   F   8.   For large volume or fast-paced operations, sautéed or griddled whole cooked sandwiches should be assembled at the last possible moment.

_____

_____

_____

Part 2

Circle the clue in parentheses that best completes each of the following statements.

9.   Hamburgers, chicken breasts, eggs, and pork chops are frequently served as (**deep-fried or griddled**) (**whole cooked**) (**sautéed or griddled**) ingredients for hot sandwiches.

10.   Checking the finished cooked product for a meat or fish sandwich with an instant-read thermometer is (**acceptable but unnecessary**) (**a good idea**) (**essential**).

11.   Steaks can be cooked to a lesser degree than hamburger meat because *E. coli* is (**located on the surface of**) (**unable to live on**) a solid piece of meat.

12.   Deep-fried ingredients have the advantage of adding (**crunch**) (**concentrated heat**) (**moisture**) to a hot sandwich.

13.   If it is necessary to hold deep-fried ingredients, hold them (**covered**) (**uncovered**) in a warmer.

14.   Deep-fried sandwiches have a higher fat content and therefore, (**benefit from**) (**are unsuitable for**) spicy, acidic, and fresh condiments.

(Continued)

Activity A *(Continued)*   **Name** _____

15. Catfish, oysters, chicken breast, and falafel are some common (**griddled**) (**sautéed**) (**poached**) (**deep-fried**) sandwich ingredients.

16. Poaching is (**rarely**) (**often**) used to cook or heat hot sandwich ingredients.

17. (**Poaching**) (**Boiling**) is the best cooking method for sausages.

18. Grilled cheese sandwiches really are (**grilled**) (**sautéed or griddled**) (**toasted**).

19. A tool for cooking sandwiches that consists of two hot, smooth surfaces that close on the top and bottom of the sandwich is called a (**panini grill**) (**clamshell griddle**).

20. A tool for cooking sandwiches that consists of two hot surfaces with ridges that leave grill marks on the cooked sandwich is called a (**panini grill**) (**clamshell griddle**).

21. The most well-known example of a whole deep-fried sandwich is the (**tuna melt**) (**Monte Cristo**).

22. Whole baked sandwiches that are wrapped before cooking produce a (**more flavorful**) (**drier**) sandwich.

Making Pizza

Chapter 33

Activity B

Name _____

Date _____ Period _____

Part 1

Read each statement below. Circle the letter *T* if the statement is true. If the statement is false, circle *F* and write the corrected statement on the lines that follow.

T   F   1.   Pizza is a flatbread that is cooked in a hot oven with an assortment of toppings.

_____

_____

T   F   2.   Pizza dough is significantly different from bread dough.

_____

_____

T   F   3.   A pizza peel is a large spatula used to spread toppings on pizza.

_____

_____

T   F   4.   Thin crust pizza will have a crisp crust if it is baked directly on the oven floor or on a perforated pizza pan.

_____

_____

T   F   5.   Deep-dish pizza and thin crust pizza both begin with a circle of pizza dough.

_____

_____

T   F   6.   Deep-dish pizza is always baked directly on the oven floor in a moderate oven.

_____

_____

(Continued)

Activity A *(Continued)*   **Name** _____

Part 2

Circle the clue in parentheses that best completes each of the following statements.

7. Deep-dish pizza dough is rolled (**thicker than**) (**thinner than**) (**the same thickness as**) thin crust pizza dough is rolled.

8. Deep-dish pizza dough is rolled out several inches (**smaller**) (**larger**) than the size of the deep-dish pizza pan.

9. The cheese of choice for pizza is (**Parmesan**) (**American**) (**mozzarella**).

10. The sequence for adding toppings to pizza after the dough has been rolled out is
    (**grated cheese, other toppings, then tomato sauce**)
    (**tomato sauce, cheese, then other toppings**)
    (**tomato sauce, other toppings, then cheese**).

Dairy and Egg Identification

34

Culinary Terminology

Name _____

Date _____Period_____

Match the following terms and identifying statements. Terms may be used more than once.

_____ 1. An ingredient that causes milk to thicken dramatically when making cheese.

_____ 2. The watery portion of milk that contains one type of protein in milk.

_____ 3. Process that permanently and evenly distributes the butterfat in milk.

_____ 4. Process that involves heating milk to a specific temperature for a specific length of time to kill pathogens.

_____ 5. Rennet is an example of this type of ingredient.

_____ 6. A term for trays that hold 30 eggs.

_____ 7. Rapid mixing of cream that produces butter.

_____ 8. A type of pasteurization.

_____ 9. Part of milk that contains the casein proteins.

_____ 10. The main carbohydrate in milk.

_____ 11. This is placed in a mold and, as it ages, knits together to form cheese.

_____ 12. Also called a sugar, although it is not sweet to taste.

A. churning

B. coagulant

C. curds

D. flats

E. homogenization

F. lactose

G. pasteurization

H. ultra high temperature (UHT)

I. whey

Using Technology to Alter Milk Composition

Chapter 34

Activity B

Name _____

Date _____Period_____

Part 1: Basic Composition of Milk

Complete the pictograph below by dividing the "glass of whole milk" into sections that represent the percentage of each component found in milk. Complete the callout labels and draw an arrow from each label to the corresponding section of the graph.

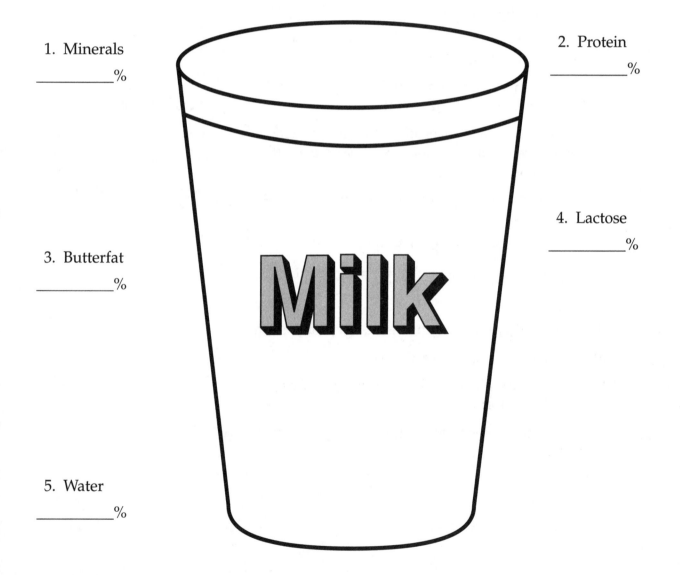

1. Minerals

_____%

2. Protein

_____%

4. Lactose

_____%

3. Butterfat

_____%

5. Water

_____%

(Continued)

Activity B *(Continued)*   **Name** _____

Part 2: Changing Butterfat Content

Read each statement below. Circle the letter *T* if the statement is true. If the statement is false, circle *F* and write the corrected statement on the lines that follow.

T   F   6.   A centrifuge spins milk at high speeds to separate the butterfat from the rest of milk.

_____

_____

T   F   7.   All the butterfat is removed from milk before it is sold.

_____

_____

T   F   8.   Both milk and high butterfat products are defined by their levels of butterfat.

_____

_____

T   F   9.   Removed butterfat is discarded.

_____

_____

Part 3: Changing Concentration

Match the following terms and identifying statements. Answer the questions that follow.

_____ 10.   Milk that has 60 percent of the water removed and a large amount of sugar added. A thick, rich, very sweet product that is canned and commonly used in baked products.

A.   dried milk powder

B.   evaporated milk

C.   sweetened condensed milk

_____ 11.   Milk that has 60 percent of the water removed. This thick, rich product is sold canned.

_____ 12.   Skim milk that has nearly all of the water removed during a drying process. The resulting white powder does not require refrigeration and has a long shelf life.

(Continued)

Activity B *(Continued)*   **Name** _____

13. What effect does removing water from milk have on the level of protein in the milk?

   _____

   _____

14. What effect does removing water from milk have on the level of sugar in the milk?

   _____

   _____

15. What effect does removing water from milk have on the level of butterfat in the milk?

   _____

   _____

Reviewing Key Concepts

Chapter 34

Name _____

Activity C

Date _____Period_____

Part 1

Circle the clue in parentheses that best completes each of the following statements.

1. Butter is made by rapid mixing or (**pasteurization**) (**churning**) (**UHT**) of cream.

2. As the cream is mixed to make butter, lumps of (**lactose**) (**curds**) (**butterfat**) emerge and begin to stick together to form larger and larger pieces of butter.

3. A purchase form of butter that is individually wrapped, one-pound pieces is typically called (**butterfats**) (**butter prints**) (**butter sticks**).

4. Grocery stores commonly sell butter in individually wrapped, quarter-pound sticks; packed (**four**) (**six**) (**eight**) to a box and (**12**) (**24**) (**36**) boxes to a case.

5. Whipped butter is butter mixed with (**curds**) (**lactose**) (**nitrogen**) to make it fluffy.

6. Cultured dairy products are the result of adding (**friendly bacteria**) (**nitrogen**) to milk.

7. The substance that thickens a cultured dairy product during the incubation period is (**lactic acid**) (**nitrogen**) (**friendly bacteria**).

8. The color of an egg shell (**is**) (**is not**) an indication of quality.

9. Within the egg white is a twisted white cord that connects the (**yolk to the white**) (**yolk to the shell**) (**white to the shell**). The cord (**is**) (**is not**) edible.

10. The egg white of a fresh egg is (**thick**) (**thin**); the white of an old egg is (**thick**) (**thin**).

11. The egg (**white**) (**yolk**) contains most of the nutrients in an egg.

12. Eggs have an air pocket between the shell and the egg white at one end. As the egg gets older the pocket gets (**smaller**) (**larger**).

13. The most common purchase forms of eggs are
(**shell eggs, pasteurized eggs, blends, dried, and hard-boiled**)
(**shell eggs, homogenized eggs, blends, dried, and parboiled**).

14. Eggs and dairy products (**are**) (**are not**) susceptible to spoilage.

15. Dairy and egg products must be kept (**away from light**) (**under refrigeration**).

16. Eggs and dairy products (**can**) (**cannot**) absorb flavors such as onions and garlic.

17. Eggs with a crack in the shell (**are safe**) (**are not safe**) to use.

18. Buttermilk, yogurt, and sour cream are (**homogenization**) (**cultured**) dairy products.

Activity C (*Continued*)   **Name** _____

Part 2

Match the following terms and identifying statements. Some terms will be used more than once.

_____ 19. Have elastic or creamy texture. When well aged, they can become runny.

_____ 20. Also called *pasta filata*.

_____ 21. The color of these cheeses is a type of edible mold.

_____ 22. Feel firm but are still elastic, and are aged for at least a month before being sold.

_____ 23. The driest cheeses, and therefore have a very long shelf lives.

_____ 24. Begins with grated cheeses that are melted and mixed with an emulsifier, water, and sometimes additional fat.

_____ 25. High moisture cheeses that are barely aged at all.

_____ 26. Examples included Morbier, Monterey Jack, Fontina, and Colby.

_____ 27. Examples include Roquefort, Stilton, Gorgonzola, and Maytag Blue.

_____ 28. Examples include Brie, Camembert, and lightly aged goat cheeses also known as *chevre*.

_____ 29. Formed into blocks or squirted into jars.

_____ 30. Spoil more easily than other cheeses.

_____ 31. To make these cheeses, hot curds are repeatedly stretched.

_____ 32. When these cheeses become very hard, they are referred to as grating cheeses.

_____ 33. The most famous member of this family is American cheese.

_____ 34. Examples include cream cheese, cottage cheese, and ricotta.

_____ 35. Examples include mozzarella, string cheese, and Provolone.

_____ 36. Examples include Parmesan, Cheddar, Swiss, Manchego, Gruyère, and Romano.

A. blue cheeses

B. fresh cheeses

C. hard cheeses

D. medium firm cheeses

E. processed cheeses

F. soft cheeses

G. stretched cheeses

Breakfast Cookery

Culinary Terminology

Name _____

Date _____ Period _____

Match the egg preparations with the descriptions of their cooking processes.

_____ 1. The chef gently lowers two shell eggs directly into a pan of simmering water. As soon as the water returns to a simmer, the chef sets a timer to two minutes. When the timer goes off, the chef removes the eggs and places them in eggcups for service.

_____ 2. The chef breaks three eggs into a mixing bowl and whisks in a little milk, salt, and pepper. The chef heats just enough butter in a nonstick pan to coat the bottom. When the butter begins to bubble, the chef pours in the egg mixture and stirs just until the eggs began to coagulate. Once the eggs form into a cohesive mass, the chef sprinkles cheese over the top, folds the mass over to form a half circle, and places it on the serving plate.

_____ 3. The chef cracks two eggs directly into a pan of hot butter. As the eggs cook over moderate heat, the chef spoons the hot butter in the pan over the top of the eggs to lightly cook the yolks. The eggs are removed from the pan without flipping.

_____ 4. The chef soaks bread slices in a mixture of egg and milk, then fries the soaked bread on a griddle. The slices are flipped over and cooked until both sides are golden brown.

_____ 5. The chef cracks two eggs directly into a pan of hot butter. When the eggs are cooked to the desired doneness, the chef slides them out of the pan and onto a plate with the yolks facing up.

A. basted eggs

B. coddled eggs

C. eggs over

D. French toast

E. frittata

F. omelet

G. poached eggs

H. sunny-side up eggs

(Continued)

Activity A (Continued)   **Name** _____

_____ 6. The chef cracks two eggs directly into a pan of hot butter and cooks them just until the whites are fully coagulated. Then the chef carefully flips the eggs over and continues to cook them to the doneness ordered by the customer.

_____ 7. The chef breaks three eggs into a mixing bowl and whisks in a little milk, salt, pepper, and herbs. The chef pours the egg mixture into a nonstick pan containing a small amount of hot butter. The chef stirs just until the eggs began to coagulate. When the eggs form a cohesive mass and brown, the chef flips the mass to allow the topside to brown. When top and bottom are browned, the chef slides the egg mass onto the serving plate without folding.

_____ 8. The chef cracks an egg into a small bowl and lowers the egg carefully into gently boiling water to which some vinegar has been added. The chef uses a slotted spoon to swirl the egg to form a round shape with the white enveloping the yolk. After three minutes, the chef uses the slotted spoon to lift the egg from the water and into a serving bowl.

A. basted eggs

B. coddled eggs

C. eggs over

D. French toast

E. frittata

F. omelet

G. poached eggs

H. sunny-side up eggs

Cooking Breakfast Meats

Chapter 35

Name _____

Activity B

Date _____ Period_____

Circle the clue in parentheses that best completes each of the following statements.

1. Ham is best (**quickly**) (**slowly**) panfried or grilled to keep it moist and tender.

2. Breakfast sausage is made (**only from pork**) (**from pork, chicken, and turkey**) (**from beef, chicken, and pork**).

3. Sausage links (**have**) (**do not have**) casings.

4. Sausage patties (**have**) (**do not have**) casings.

5. In most commercial kitchens, bacon is cooked (**by panfrying**) (**by grilling**) (**in the oven**).

6. Breakfast sausages are (**panfried**) (**deep fried**) or grilled until done.

7. Nicely shaped strips and even cooking are two advantages of cooking bacon (**by panfrying**) (**by grilling**) (**in the oven**).

8. Regardless of how crisp the final product will be, bacon should be cooked until (**the red is very dark**) (**the strip is no longer shiny**) (**no white fat is visible**).

9. Professional kitchens often prepare breakfast sausage (**by deep frying**) (**by broiling**) (**in the oven**).

10. Canadian bacon is (**thick bacon**) (**thin ham**) (**boneless pork loin**).

11. Canadian bacon is cooked the same as (**bacon**) (**ham**).

12. Breakfast sausages should be cooked (**rare**) (**medium**) (**well-done**).

13. Many commercial kitchens purchase bacon that is already (**cut into bite-sized lengths**) (**laid out on ovenproof parchment paper**) (**separated into serving size portions**).

14. Professional cooks frequently cook ham (**by broiling**) (**by steaming**) (**in the oven**).

Reviewing Key Concepts

Chapter 35

Activity C

Name _____

Date _____ Period_____

Part 1: Breakfast Batters

Read each statement below. Circle the letter *T* if the statement is true. If the statement is false, circle *F* and write the corrected statement on the lines that follow.

T   F   1.   The batter for French toast is a mixture of eggs, milk, and fat.

_____

_____

T   F   2.   Pancakes are a form of quick bread that is baked in the oven.

_____

_____

T   F   3.   Pancakes are leavened with yeast.

_____

_____

T   F   4.   Overmixing pancake batter can result in dense or tough pancakes.

_____

_____

T   F   5.   Turn pancakes when bubbles appear on the surface and the bottom is still white.

_____

_____

T   F   6.   Pancakes must be served as soon as possible, because they may become dry and flat if held over a period of time.

_____

_____

(Continued)

Activity C (*Continued*)   **Name** _____

T   F   7. Waffles are a quick bread that has a batter that is a little thinner and contains less fat than pancake batter.

_____

_____

T   F   8. The batter for French toast can be varied by adding different flavorings to the batter.

_____

_____

T   F   9. To assure that waffles are crisp and don't stick, start waffle in a cold waffle iron.

_____

_____

Part 2: Hot Cereals

Read each statement below. Circle the letter *T* if the statement is true. If the statement is false, circle *F* and write the corrected statement on the lines that follow.

T   F   10. The proper ratio of liquid to cereal and the amount of time needed for cooking is essentially the same for all types of cereal grains.

_____

_____

T   F   11. Cereal should be cooked until it is dry.

_____

_____

T   F   12. Once placed in a steam table, the consistency of hot cereal will hold for hours.

_____

_____

T   F   13. Hot cereals are a nutritious source of B vitamins and fat.

_____

_____

(Continued)

Activity C (*Continued*)   **Name** _____

T F   14. Farina is a cereal made from processed rice.

_____

_____

T F   15. Grits is a cereal made from ground wheat.

_____

_____

T F   16. Steel cut oatmeal has a finer texture and requires less cooking time than rolled oats.

_____

_____

T F   17. Rice cereals that are cracked are typically cooked to a smooth consistency.

_____

_____

Introduction to the Bakeshop

Culinary Terminology

Chapter 36

Activity A

Name _____

Date _____ Period _____

Match the following terms and identifying statements.

_____ 1. The head of the baking and pastry department.

_____ 2. The process in which yeast, in a warm moist environment, feeds on carbohydrates and gives off carbon dioxide and alcohol.

_____ 3. The term often used to refer to fats used in the bakeshop.

_____ 4. Food professional who prepares and bakes breads.

_____ 5. An alkaline powder, also known as *sodium bicarbonate,* used as a chemical leavener.

_____ 6. A process in which gases are trapped in dough creating small bubbles that give baked goods a light and airy texture.

_____ 7. A mixture of equal parts of water and sugar by weight that is brought to a boil and simmered just until the sugar dissolves in the water.

_____ 8. A chemical leavener that is sodium bicarbonate premixed with an acid chemical, such as cream of tartar.

_____ 9. A rubbery substance that is responsible for giving baked goods structure.

_____ 10. Food professional responsible for preparing sweet dessert items.

_____ 11. Alcohol-based flavorings.

A. baker

B. baking powder

C. baking soda

D. extracts

E. fermentation

F. gluten

G. leavening

H. pastry chef

I. pastry cook

J. shortening

K. simple syrup

The Chemistry of Baking

Chapter 36   Name _____

Activity B   Date _____Period_____

Circle the clue in parentheses that best completes each of the following statements.

1. The main difference between the various types of flour used in the bakeshop is the (**sugar**) (**protein**) content of the flours.

2. When flour is mixed with water, the (**sugar**) (**protein**) in the flour produces gluten.

3. In professional bakeshops, wheat flours are categorized by their (**sugar**) (**gluten**) potential.

4. In addition to adding a sweet taste, sugar helps maintain (**color**) (**moistness**) in cakes.

5. Sugar assists in the (**mixing**) (**leavening**) process in breads.

6. Sugar is used to make cookies (**soft**) (**crisp**).

7. Fat (**lengthens**) (**shortens**) strands of gluten in dough, making the product (**less**) (**more**) tender and (**more**) (**less**) elastic or chewy.

8. Shortenings add flavor, color, and (**moisture**) (**density**) to baked goods.

9. The decision of which shortening to use for a given application is based on its (**oiliness**) (**melting point**) and nutritional content.

10. Baking soda is an (**acidic**) (**alkaline**) powder used as a (**chemical**) (**yeast**) leavening agent.

11. Baking powder is (**flour**) (**baking soda**) premixed with an (**acid**) (**alkaline**) chemical.

12. Milk, buttermilk, cocoa, molasses, and cream of tartar are ingredients that can provide the (**acid**) (**alkaline**) needed for (**baking soda**) (**baking powder**) to release carbon dioxide gas.

13. Yeast is a (**chemical**) (**living microscopic plant**) (**living microscopic animal**) used to leaven bread and some baked goods.

14. (**Compressed yeast**) (**Dry yeast**) is a fresh product with a limited shelf life and should be refrigerated.

(Continued)

Activity B *(Continued)*   Name _____

15. The quality of chocolate products is measured by their
    (**flavor, smell, appearance, texture, and melting point**)
    (**flavor, texture, and melting point**) (**flavor, appearance, texture, and graininess**).

16. Chocolate liquor is composed of cocoa solids and fat called (**cocoa liquor**) (**cocoa beans**)
    (**cocoa butter**).

17. When stored in conditions of fluctuating temperature or humidity, chocolate can
    develop a (**black**) (**white**) (**blue**) film on its surface. For this reason (**always**) (**never**)
    store chocolate in the refrigerator.

18. Most pastry chefs prefer (**powdered**) (**sheet**) gelatin because it is easier to use.

19. Gelatin is used to (**sweeten**) (**thicken**) (**smooth**) various sweet and savory preparations.

20. The first step in using gelatin is called (**blooming**) (**melting**) (**coloring**), which means to
    soften gelatin in cold water.

21. Softened gelatin is melted or dissolved in a small amount of (**fat**) (**liquid**) (**leavening**).

22. To soften powdered gelatin, mix with about (**two**) (**four**) (**six**) times its weight in cold
    water.

23. Store nuts in tightly sealed containers in a (**warm**) (**cool**) place.

24. Generally, the larger the nut pieces, the (**less**) (**more**) expensive they are.

25. Nuts (**can**) (**cannot**) be frozen for long term storage.

26. Seeds are rich in (**sugar**) (**fat**).

27. Seeds develop a (**richer**) (**flatter**) taste when toasted.

28. Alcohol-based flavorings are called (**pastes**) (**extracts**).

29. Flavorings and extracts have (**mild**) (**strong**) flavors.

30. Artificial vanilla is made from a synthetic compound called (**vanilla bean**) (**vanillin**).

Reviewing Key Concepts

Chapter 36

Activity C

Name _____

Date _____ Period _____

Part 1: Smallwares and Hand Tools

Match the following terms and identifying statements.

_____ 1. Rectangular pans used for baking bread.

_____ 2. Knives with thin flexible blades of various lengths and widths. They are used for spreading frostings and also as spatulas to pick up or turn items.

_____ 3. A piece of metal or plastic with a zigzag edge that is dragged through pastry coating or frosting to give it a decorative texture.

_____ 4. Shallow round pans often with fluted sides; most with removable bottoms.

_____ 5. A large, long-handled paddle used to slide baked goods in and out of deep ovens.

_____ 6. Cone-shaped bag made of cloth or plastic that has a small opening at the point of the cone into which a metal tip is placed. The bag is filled with product that is squeezed through the tip to create a decorative effect.

_____ 7. Also referred to as *baking sheets*. The sides are sometimes extended by using a 3-inch-high frame.

_____ 8. Two platforms, an ingredient scoop, and a counterweight to balance the scoop.

_____ 9. A single piece, either cylindrical or thin with tapered ends, that is used to roll pieces of dough into thin sheets.

_____ 10. Device that allows pastry cooks to frost a cake by holding a palette knife loaded with frosting stationary alongside the cake and while spinning the cake.

_____ 11. Round pans with straight sides used for baking cakes.

_____ 12. Deep cake pans with sides made of a flexible band of metal that can be opened up. These pans are used for cakes and pastries that might be hard to remove from a standard cake pan.

_____ 13. Sets of small round pans pressed into a single sheet of metal. Used for cupcakes or muffins.

A. baker's peel

B. balance scale

C. cake pans

D. loaf pans

E. muffin pans

F. palette knife

G. pastry bag

H. pastry comb

I. rolling pin

J. sheet pans

K. spring form pans

L. tart pans

M. turntable

(Continued)

Activity C *(Continued)*   **Name** _____

Part 2: Large Equipment

Match the following terms and identifying statements.

_____ 14. Sometimes called *roll-in ovens*, are large enough to hold an entire sheet pan rack. The rack is loaded with items to be baked and then rolled into the oven. The products are baked on the rack.

_____ 15. An oven with a deep, wide cavity with a height of about 10 inches. Each oven is capable of holding several sheet pans. Heat can be controlled from the bottom, top, and sides for different baking effects.

_____ 16. The three basic attachments for this appliance are the whip, paddle, and dough hook.

_____ 17. A cabinet that will hold dough products at a warm temperature so they will rise.

_____ 18. A mechanized rolling pin. The thickness of the rollers can be adjusted.

_____ 19. These ovens have a series of trays set up in a Ferris wheel-like arrangement. As items are baking, the trays revolve inside the oven to allow all of the items to bake evenly.

_____ 20. Essentially a refrigerated drum with a blade or paddle that spins inside it. Slowly turns liquid mixture into a frozen solid.

_____ 21. A press that evenly divides a preweighed amount of dough into many smaller portions for rolls or buns.

A. deck ovens

B. dough divider

C. dough sheeter

D. ice-cream machines

E. mixers

F. proofers

G. rack ovens

H. revolving ovens

Quick Breads and Batters

Culinary Terminology

Name _____

Date _____ Period_____

Match the following terms and identifying statements. Terms may be used more than once.

_____ 1. During the last step of this process, gluten develops and the leavening agent reacts.

_____ 2. Individual fried pastry.

_____ 3. The paste or thick batter used to make cream puffs and éclairs.

_____ 4. Combines dry ingredients first; then solid shortening is cut in, and finally, liquid ingredients are added and mixed just enough to combine with the other ingredients.

_____ 5. A mixture of flour and other ingredients that is stiff enough to form into shapes for baking.

_____ 6. May be formed from a dough or from a batter.

_____ 7. A very thin pancake.

_____ 8. A mixture of flour and enough liquid so that the mixture is pourable.

_____ 9. Is one of the few pastry preparations made on the stove top.

_____ 10. Chemically leavened baked product.

_____ 11. Muffins, pancakes, waffles, and cream puffs all begin as this.

_____ 12. Requires no leavening agent because it is paper-thin.

_____ 13. One characteristic this type of product has is soft texture; many contain a good amount of shortening, which helps create a tender product.

A. batter

B. biscuit method

C. crêpe

D. dough

E. fritter

F. pâte à choux

G. quick bread

The Basics of Quick Breads and Batters

Chapter 37   Name _____

Activity B   Date _____Period_____

Circle the clue in parentheses that best completes each of the following statements.

1. Quick breads are leavened with chemical leaveners such as baking powder or baking soda; both of which act (**more quickly**) (**more slowly**) than yeast.

2. Quick breads begin in the form of (**dough**) (**batter**) (**either dough or batter**).

3. Quality quick breads are (**dense and chewy**) (**dry and flaky**) (**light and tender**).

4. Quick bread dough is often (**high**) (**low**) in moisture.

5. One ingredient used in quick bread recipes that contributes to its delicate texture is (**low**) (**balanced**) (**high**) gluten flour.

6. One ingredient used in quick bread recipes that contributes to its delicate texture is the (**limited**) (**good**) amount of shortening.

7. The manner in which the dough is prepared (**is very important**) (**is not really important**) in trying to achieve a tender texture.

8. The proportion of liquid to flour in a batter is (**the same as**) (**greater than**) (**less than**) the proportion of liquid to flour in dough.

9. Mixing (**develops**) (**hinders**) gluten in the flour of a dough.

10. Overmixing results in (**too little**) (**too much**) gluten; making the finished product (**dense and chewy**) (**dry and flaky**) (**light and tender**).

11. Most quick breads are mixed (**until all ingredients are well combined and smooth**) (**only to the point necessary to combine ingredients**).

12. Holes or tunnels inside products or poorly shaped products are likely the result of (**undermixing**) (**overmixing**).

Reviewing Key Concepts

Chapter 37

Activity C

Name _____

Date _____ Period _____

Part 1: Types of Quick Breads

Match the following terms and identifying statements.

_____ 1. A savory quick bread that can be served at any meal. Some bakers demand special low gluten, high starch content flours made from soft wheat to ensure a light flaky product.

_____ 2. Small, individual fried pastries.

_____ 3. A quick bread popular throughout Great Britain that is leavened with baking powder or baking soda and commonly cut into a triangle shape before baking.

_____ 4. Individual pastries similar to cupcakes.

_____ 5. Is essentially a form of another quick bread but uses cornmeal as the main ingredient.

A. biscuits

B. cornbread

C. fritters

D. muffins

E. scones

Part 2: Techniques for Preparing Quick Breads

Circle the clue in parentheses that best completes each of the following statements.

6. The method for mixing biscuit dough is fairly consistent. It calls for **(adding liquid ingredients to dry ingredients, then cutting in shortening)** **(combining dry ingredients, cutting in shortening, then adding liquid ingredients)** **(adding shortening to liquid ingredients, then combining with dry ingredients)**.

7. Biscuit dough can be portioned into individual biscuits by **(using a scoop to form clumps of dough)** **(rolling the dough and cutting it into individual rounds)** **(scooping or rolling and cutting)**.

8. Biscuits should be placed on **(greased)** **(ungreased)** sheet pans to bake.

9. When preparing muffins, **(add liquid ingredients to dry ingredients and then cut in shortening)** **(combine dry ingredients, cut in shortening, and then add liquid ingredients)** **(add shortening to liquid ingredients and then add that mixture to dry ingredients)** and mix to combine.

10. Fritters are formed from dough that is **(yeast raised)** **(a quick bread)** **(yeast raised or quick bread)**.

11. Fritters are **(fried)** **(baked)** **(cooked on a griddle)**.

(Continued)

Activity C *(Continued)*   **Name** _____

Part 3: Other Products That Begin as Batters

Circle the clue in parentheses that best completes each of the following statements.

12. The paste or thick batter used to make cream puffs and éclairs is **(crêpes)** **(pâte à choux)**.

13. Chefs need to add no leavening to **(crêpes)** **(pâte à choux)** **(crêpes nor pâte à choux)**.

14. Crêpes are made **(with)** **(without)** **(with or without)** sugar.

15. The following technique is for making **(crêpes)** **(pâte à choux)** **(crêpes or pâte à choux)** batter: First combine the liquid, fat, sugar, and salt in a saucepot and bring to a boil. Add all the flour at once and stir immediately. Cook over moderate heat while stirring until the batter forms a ball and pulls away from the sides of the pot.

16. The following technique is for making **(crêpes)** **(pâte à choux)** **(crêpes or pâte à choux)** batter: Combine the dry ingredients, beat in the eggs, add liquid gradually. Strain to remove any lumps.

17. **(Crêpes)** **(Pâte à choux)** are cooked in a pan.

18. Eggs are added one at a time when preparing **(crêpes)** **(pâte à choux)**.

19. Steam helps to leaven **(crêpes)** **(pâte à choux)**.

20. Products made from batters for **(crêpes)** **(pâte à choux)** **(crêpes and pâte à choux)** can be filled with either sweet or savory fillings.

Cookies

Cookie Conversations

Chapter 38

Activity A

Name _____

Date _____ Period_____

Fragments of conversation that might be overheard in a professional kitchen are listed in the left column of the chart below. Place a check (✓) in column that corresponds with the classification of cookie being discussed.

	Classification of Cookie					
	Bar	Drop	Icebox	Rolled	Sheet	Spritz
"The production sheet says to make 12 dozen each checkerboard and pinwheel cookies for the catered event today."						
"We need to standardize the new recipe for multilayered cookies with dates, nuts, and jam."						
"Please get out the large and medium sized rosette disks."						
"Portion the dough into one-pound batches and form it into a log about the length of this sheet pan."						
"After you frost these brownies, cut them into 2-inch squares."						
"Now shape the dough into a triangle, wrap it in plastic wrap and put it in the refrigerator to chill."						
"Use the #16 portion scoop so that all of the mounds will be the same size, and be sure to leave room for the cookies to flatten out as they bake."						
"These cookies are sliced and ready for their second baking."						
"Roll the dough a little thinner before you cut it into shapes."						
"Use the pastry bag to prepare the star-shaped cookies for the catering."						
"We need four dozen chocolate chip cookies and two dozen oatmeal."						
"Please prepare two pounds of buttercream icing for these sugar cookies."						

Reviewing Key Concepts

Chapter 38

Activity B

Name _____

Date _____ Period _____

Part 1: Characteristics of a Quality Cookie

Circle the clue in parentheses that best completes each of the following statements.

1. The flavor of cookies is mostly determined by the (**baking time**) (**quality of the ingredients**) (**decorating techniques**).

2. The texture of cookies is mostly determined by (**baking time**) (**ingredients**) (**decorating techniques**).

3. Baking (**at the proper temperature and for the proper time**) (**at the proper temperature**) (**for the proper time**) is essential for proper color of cookies.

4. Choosing (**high-gluten**) (**low-gluten**) flour can make cookies tough.

5. Flavor of cookies (**is**) (**is not**) affected by how fresh the ingredients are.

6. Uniform-shaped cookies (**is**) (**is not**) key to the appearance of quality cookies.

7. The more sugar added to the dough, the (**less crisp**) (**more crisp**) the cookies will be.

8. To ensure good appearance, remove cookies from the sheet as soon as they (**come out of the oven**) (**have had a chance to firm up**).

9. Careful measurement of ingredients (**is**) (**is not**) essential to achieve good cookie flavor.

10. Spending extra time mixing cookie dough causes (**more**) (**less**) gluten to develop; making the finished product (**tough**) (**light and tender**).

11. Decorating cookies uniformly is important to creating attractive cookies because (**finished cookies will taste alike**) (**cookies are often displayed in batches**).

12. Proper proportions of dough ingredients (**are**) (**are not**) necessary to achieve a pleasing flavor of quality cookies.

Part 2: Common Methods of Mixing Cookie Dough

Read each statement below. Circle the letter *T* if the statement is true. If the statement is false, circle *F* and write the corrected statement on the lines that follow.

T   F   13. The creaming method is the simplest way to make cookie dough.

_____

_____

(Continued)

Activity B (*Continued*)   **Name** _____

T F   14. The first step in the creaming method is to put all the ingredients into a bowl.

_____

_____

T F   15. Both the one-stage method and the creaming method are done with an electric mixer using the paddle attachment.

_____

_____

T F   16. Allow five to six minutes at moderate speed to fully blend all ingredients in the one-stage method.

_____

_____

T F   17. In the creaming method, butter is mixed with sugar just until moist.

_____

_____

T F   18. One advantage of the creaming method is that it is less likely to overdevelop gluten.

_____

_____

T F   19. One advantage of the one-stage method is that it is less likely to overdevelop gluten.

_____

_____

T F   20. In the creaming method ingredients are mixed in the following sequence: butter is mixed with sugar; spices and liquids are added next; flour is added third; and eggs are dropped in one at a time, last.

_____

_____

Common Methods for Forming Cookies

Chapter 38

Activity C

Name _____

Date _____ Period_____

Cookies are often classified by the method used to form the dough into a cookie. On the space provided before each of the descriptions below, write *bar, drop, icebox, rolled, sheet,* or *spritz* to indicate the method used to form the cookies.

_____ 1. Dough is rolled into a thin sheet and various shaped cutters are used to cut out the cookies. The cookie shapes are placed on a sheet pan and baked.

_____ 2. A scoop is used to portion dough that is placed onto a sheet pan with enough space between for the cookies to spread during cooking.

_____ 3. Cookie dough is portioned into approximately one-pound (454 g) batches and formed into logs about the length of a sheet pan. Each log is flattened and baked. When it is cooked, and still warm, the logs are sliced into one-inch (2-cm) segments to form cookies, which are baked a second time to create a hard texture.

_____ 4. Cookie batter or dough is evenly spread onto a sheet pan and baked. Later the sheet is cut into individual cookies.

_____ 5. Cookie dough is formed into a log, triangle, or other shape and then wrapped in plastic wrap or parchment paper and refrigerated. When the dough is fully chilled, it is sliced into individual cookies and baked.

_____ 6. Soft cookie dough is forced through a pastry bag to form individual shapes such as rosettes, shells, and scrolls or the dough is pressed through a specially shaped die on a cookie press.

Culinary Terminology

Chapter 39

Activity A

Name _____

Date _____ Period _____

Match the following terms and identifying statements. Terms may be used more than once.

_____ 1. Step in the process that comes after the dough has risen the first time.

_____ 2. Portioning dough by weight.

_____ 3. Repeatedly folding and pressing the dough after it is mixed.

_____ 4. The act of cutting small slashes in the surface of risen dough.

_____ 5. The process in which yeast dough is allowed to rise after it is shaped and before it is baked.

_____ 6. The process by which carbohydrates are consumed by yeast, and alcohol and carbon dioxide are released.

_____ 7. The part of yeast product preparation that is done to develop gluten.

_____ 8. This process allows gases to escape during the baking process and also create a decorative pattern on the surface of the finished loaf.

_____ 9. The process involving the consumption of carbohydrates by a living organism.

_____ 10. This process can happen by placing unbaked bread in a special box or by covering it with a cloth and placing it in a warm place.

_____ 11. For small quantities of dough, this step can be done by hand; large quantities are usually processed on the mixer with the dough hook.

_____ 12. The name of this step is not to be taken literally.

A. docking

B. fermentation

C. kneading

D. proofing

E. punching

F. scaling

The Science of Yeast-Raised Products

Chapter 39

Activity B

Name _____

Date _____ Period _____

Part 1: Temperature

Circle the clue in parentheses that best completes each of the following statements.

1. Dissolving yeast in liquids at temperatures over 138°F (59°C) is not recommended because the yeast **(will still work but much more slowly)** **(could be killed and not work at all)**.

2. Bakers create proper conditions for fermentation by adjusting the temperature of the **(room) (flour) (liquid)**.

3. Fermentation is best done in a **(cool) (warm) (hot)** place with no drafts.

4. The temperature in a proof box is typically around **(78°F to 82°F [26°C to 28°C])** **(100°F [38°C]) (138°F [59C°])**.

5. Breads are baked at varying temperatures and various times depending on their size and **(the amount of gluten in the flour) (the desired crispness of the finished product)**.

6. Refrigeration causes baked bread to **(remain fresh longer) (become stale more quickly)**.

Part 2: Gluten

7. Gluten is the **(carbohydrate) (fat) (protein)** that gives dough its structure and elasticity.

8. The more dough is kneaded; the **(more) (less)** gluten is developed.

9. How long and at what speed dough is kneaded affects gluten development which, in turn, affects the **(crispness) (sweetness) (texture)** of the finished product.

Part 3: Fermentation

10. Fermentation can take as long as **(one and a half hours) (two and a half hours)** **(three and a half hours)**.

11. When fermentation is complete, the dough is punched to **(stop the gluten)** **(release carbon dioxide gas) (reactivate the yeast)**.

Part 4: Proofing

12. The steam or humidity in the proof box prevents a dry crust from forming on the dough, which would **(keep it from rising) (allow it to over rise)**.

13. Washing proofed bread with beaten egg will produce a **(pale yellow, bright)** **(golden, dull) (deep brown, glossy)** finish to the crust.

Reviewing Key Concepts

Chapter 39

Activity C

Name _____

Date _____ Period _____

Part 1: Preparing the Dough

Letter the steps for preparing dough for yeast-raised products below in sequential order. The first step should be labeled *A*.

_____ 1. Allow the dough to ferment.

_____ 2. Bake.

_____ 3. Weigh ingredients.

_____ 4. Dissolve yeast in liquid.

_____ 5. Knead the dough.

_____ 6. Mix in dry ingredients.

_____ 7. Proof the dough.

_____ 8. Punch the dough.

_____ 9. Scale the dough.

_____ 10. Shape the dough.

Part 2: Shaping Yeast Breads

Indicate whether each of the classic shapes for yeast-raised products listed below is a loaf or a roll by circling the correct term.

Classic Dough Shapes				
Shape	**(Circle one)**		**Shape**	**(Circle one)**
Bagel	(loaf)	(roll)	**Knot, figure eight**	(loaf) (roll)
Baguette	(loaf)	(roll)	**Knot, single**	(loaf) (roll)
Boule	(loaf)	(roll)	**Pan**	(loaf) (roll)
Cloverleaf	(loaf)	(roll)	**Pullman**	(loaf) (roll)
Club	(loaf)	(roll)	**Ring**	(loaf) (roll)
Crescent	(loaf)	(roll)	**Round**	(loaf) (roll)
Kaiser	(loaf)	(roll)	**Rye**	(loaf) (roll)
Knot, double	(loaf)	(roll)		

(Continued)

Activity C *(Continued)*   **Name** _____

Part 3: Proofing and Baking

Circle the clue in parentheses that best completes each of the following statements.

11. Proofing is complete when (**the dough doubles in size**)
    (**the end size of the product is reached**) (**two and a half hours have passed**).

12. When proofing is complete, the dough may be coated with a liquid to (**stop the gluten**)
    (**give the dough a particular color or create a textured crust**)
    (**to add to the taste of the product**).

13. Docking at the end of proofing creates a decorative pattern on a finished loaf and also
    allows (**the crust on soft crust breads to keep its shape**)
    (**gases to escape on hard crust breads during the baking process**).

14. At the (**beginning**) (**middle**) (**end**) of the baking process, the dough rises due to the
    expansion of the gases present in the dough.

15. During the baking process, yeast is (**activated**) (**stabilized**) (**killed**).

16. During the baking process, moisture in the dough (**evaporates**) (**condenses**) (**increases**).

17. During the baking process, starches and gluten in the dough (**evaporate**) (**become soft**)
    (**become firm**).

Pies and Tarts

40

Culinary Terminology

Chapter 40

Activity A

Name _____

Date _____ Period _____

Match the following terms and identifying statements. Terms may be used more than once.

_____ 1. A very flaky dough made by a process that creates over 1,000 extremely thin layers of dough and fat.

_____ 2. A commercially prepared product made from fruit jelly and gelatin.

_____ 3. Also called *pâte sucrée*.

_____ 4. Prebaking a pie or tart shell.

_____ 5. Dough in which the fat is cut into the flour until it has the texture of cornmeal.

_____ 6. Also called *pâte brisée*.

_____ 7. Dough in which the fat is cut into the flour until it is in pieces approximately the size of a pea.

_____ 8. Has the richest taste and flakiest texture of all baked goods.

_____ 9. Pie and tart shells are typically weighted down during this process.

_____ 10. Is the best choice of dough for pies with liquid fillings.

_____ 11. A dough used for savory tarts.

_____ 12. Dough that contains sugar and egg yolks and may contain flavorings such as ground nuts.

A. blind baking

B. flaky pie dough

C. mealy pie dough

D. pastry glaze

E. puff pastry

F. short dough

G. sweet dough

Preparing Quality Dough for Pies and Tarts

Chapter 40   **Name** _____

Activity B   **Date** _____ **Period** _____

Circle the clue in parentheses that best completes each of the following statements.

1. Most bakers use pastry flour for piecrusts because pastry flour is
    (**lower in gluten and higher in starch**) (**higher in gluten and lower in starch**)
    (**lower in gluten and lower in starch**) (**higher in gluten and higher in starch**).

2. The key to choosing the best fat for creating excellent texture is the (**weight**)
    (**melting point**) (**liquidity**) of the fat.

3. The best fat for creating flaky texture in the finished pie is (**liquid fat**) (**solid shortening**).

4. Crusts made with butter are (**more flaky than**) (**just as flaky as**) (**not as flaky as**) crusts
    made with shortening.

5. It is important that the liquid used in pie dough be (**hot**) (**lukewarm**) (**cool**) (**ice cold**).

6. To make flaky pie dough, the fat is mixed or cut into the flour until it
    (**resembles the texture of cornmeal**) (**is in pieces about the size of a pea**).

7. To make mealy pie dough, the fat is mixed or cut into the flour until it
    (**resembles the texture of cornmeal**) (**is in pieces about the size of a pea**).

8. All types of pie dough should not be overworked to avoid developing (**too much**)
    (**too little**) gluten.

9. When rolling out dough, make sure the temperature of the dough is (**hot**) (**warm**) (**cold**).

10. When you are making multiple pies, it (**is**) (**is not**) a good idea to roll out more than one
    crust at a time.

11. About (**six**) (**nine**) (**twelve**) ounces of dough is enough to line a standard nine-inch pie
    pan.

12. Dough is typically rolled out to about (**¹⁄₁₆-inch**) (**⅛-inch**) (**¼-inch**) thickness.

13. Dough is dusted with flour during rolling to keep the dough (**dry**)
    (**from sticking**) (**from falling apart**).

14. As dough is rolled out it should (**not be turned**) (**periodically be turned 90 degrees**).

Reviewing Key Concepts

Chapter 40

Activity C

Name _____

Date _____ Period_____

Part 1: Fillings for Pies

Read each statement below. Circle the letter *T* if the statement is true. If the statement is false, circle *F* and write the corrected statement on the lines that follow.

T F 1. Most commercial operations prepare fruit filling for pies with raw fruit, which is the most traditional way of preparing fruit pies.

_____

_____

T F 2. When using cooked fillings involving delicate fruit, just the juice is sweetened and thickened on the stove top.

_____

_____

T F 3. Most liquid fillings contain no ingredient that can thicken the filling.

_____

_____

T F 4. Cream pies require baking.

_____

_____

T F 5. It is essential to use a prebaked pie shell or crumb crust pie shell for chiffon pies.

_____

_____

T F 6. Chiffon pies are essentially cream fillings to which whipped cream and butter have been added.

_____

_____

(Continued)

Activity C *(Continued)*   **Name** _____

T   F   7.   Some common examples of liquid fillings are custard, pumpkin, and Bavarian
cream.

_____

_____

T   F   8.   Mealy crusts are best for liquid fillings.

_____

_____

Part 2: Tarts

Circle the clue in parentheses that best completes each of the following statements.

9. The nature of the pastry crust for tarts is essentially the same except that tarts are
   (**shallower**) (**deeper**) than pies.

10. The classical shape for tarts is (**round**) (**oval**) (**square**) (**rectangular**).

11. Traditionally, the sides of tarts are (**straight**) (**fluted**).

12. Short dough is a dough similar to (**flaky**) (**mealy**) pie dough.

13. Sweet dough is a dough similar to (**flaky**) (**mealy**) (**short**) dough.

14. Tart dough that contains egg yolks is (**short**) (**sweet**).

15. The dough used for savory tart fillings is (**short**) (**sweet**) dough.

16. The dough used for sweet tart fillings is (**short**) (**sweet**) dough.

17. The most common filling for sweet dough tarts is (**whipped cream**) (**pastry cream**).

18. Pastry glaze is brushed on fresh fruit tart toppings to (**make it shiny**)
    (**keep the fruit from drying out**).

19. The most common flavor of pastry glaze used in bakeshops is (**cherry**) (**apple**) (**apricot**)
    (**peach**) (**orange**).

(Continued)

Activity C (*Continued*)   **Name** _____

Part 3: Puff Pastry

Answer the following questions about puff pastry in the space provided.

20. Once a basic dough made with flour, butter, and water is prepared, what steps are taken to turn the basic dough into puff pastry? _____

_____

_____

_____

21. Why do many foodservice operations buy ready-made puff pastry?_____

_____

_____

22. What kinds of fillings can be used with puff pastry? _____

_____

_____

23. How does puff pastry relate to menu items described as *en croute*? _____

_____

_____

24. How does puff pastry relate to the classic dessert *napoleon*? _____

_____

_____

Cakes

The Chemical Properties of Cake Ingredients

Chapter 41

Activity A

Name _____

Date _____ Period _____

Complete the chart by circling the function of each ingredient and indicating the specific properties that ingredient provides. Use the corresponding letters from the list that follows to complete the *Properties* column.

Cake Ingredients		
Ingredient	Function (*circle one*)	Properties (*from list*)
Egg	gives structure tenderizes	
Flour	gives structure tenderizes	
Liquid	gives structure tenderizes	
Shortening	gives structure tenderizes	
Sweetener	gives structure tenderizes	

A. Aids in gluten development when mixed with flour.

B. Adds richness to the cake, and, depending on specific product, may add flavor.

C. Acts as the main source of leavening for many cakes.

D. Helps absorb liquid, which contributes to a moist cake.

E. Helps create steam for leavening in the baking process.

F. Helps dissolve sugar.

G. Incorporates air and gives light, airy texture to product.

H. Prevents overdevelopment of gluten.

I. Its proteins coagulate trapping moisture and gases.

J. Provides a sweet taste.

K. Its starch absorbs moisture.

Classifying Cakes by Mixing Methods

Chapter 41

Activity B

Name _____

Date _____ Period _____

Cakes are typically mixed using one of two methods—*creaming* or *sponge*. Write the mixing method that best matches each description. If the statement refers to both methods, write both terms.

Description	**Mixing Method**
1. _____	Method used for cakes with a high proportion of butter or shortening.
2. _____	Begins with combining the egg products with some or all of the sugar.
3. _____	Method used for genoise.
4. _____	Starts by mixing the butter or shortening with the sugar in an electric mixer with the paddle attachment
5. _____	Leavened by air whipped into eggs in the cake formula.
6. _____	After shortening is mixed with sugar, eggs and liquid are added.
7. _____	The second step in this method is to preheat the oven and prepare cake pans.
8. _____	Eggs are added gradually in this method.
9. _____	This method is also called the *foam method*.
10. _____	Dry ingredients are added last in this method.
11. _____	In this method, eggs and sugar are whipped at high speed to incorporate air.
12. _____	In this method, liquid or melted fat is added last.
13. _____	Care must be taken to not overmix cake batter when using this method.
14. _____	Batter prepared by this method, must be portioned into pans and baked immediately.
15. _____	Eggs and sugar are beaten until they are thick and ribbonlike.
16. _____	Method used for cakes with a high proportion of eggs to flour.

Reviewing Key Concepts

Chapter 41   Name _____

Activity C   Date _____ Period_____

Part 1: Preparing a Cake Pan and Baking

Circle the clue in parentheses that best completes each of the following statements.

1. Pans can be brushed with (**solid**) (**liquid**) (**solid or liquid**) shortening and then dusted with (**flour**) (**sugar**) (**flour or sugar**). Excess dusting ingredient (**will be absorbed when**) (**should be shaken out before**) the batter is poured in.

2. An alternative to dusting is to line the pan with (**plastic wrap**) (**parchment paper**).

3. The most common method used to determine the doneness of a cake is to use a skewer or toothpick. When a skewer or toothpick is inserted into the center of a baked cake, it should come out (**with dry crumbs clinging to it**) (**with moist crumbs clinging to it**) (**clean**).

4. Bakers may test a cake for doneness by gently pressing the cake. The cake is done if (**it leaves a small indent**) (**the cake springs back**).

5. A visual sign of doneness is when the sides of the cake (**darken**) (**pull away from the sides of the pan**) (**puff over the sides of the pan**).

Part 2: Assembling and Finishing Layer Cakes

Read each statement below. Circle the letter *T* if the statement is true. If the statement is false, circle *F* and write the corrected statement on the lines that follow.

T   F   6.   Cakes should be flipped so the top of the cake is the smooth surface created from the bottom of the cake pan.

_____

_____

T   F   7.   To split cakes into layers, use a chef's knife.

_____

_____

(Continued)

Activity C (*Continued*)   **Name** _____

T F 8. Before filling the layers, it is common to brush the layers with simple syrup to create a moist cake and add sweetness.

_____

_____

T F 9. To assemble layers, a thick coating of filling should be placed on the bottom layer of cake, and the next layer should be placed on top.

_____

_____

T F 10. The most popular icings are buttercream and sour cream.

_____

_____

T F 11. A pattern is often made on the sides of a cake by holding a pastry brush against the side of the cake at an angle and applying slight pressure while rotating the turntable.

_____

_____

_____

T F 12. Crumbs of nuts, shaved chocolate, or confections may be used to decorate sides of cakes.

_____

_____

T F 13. Icings in a pastry bag are used to create patterns on cakes and around the base of cakes.

_____

_____

Custards, Foams, and Buttercreams 42

Culinary Terminology

Chapter 42

Activity A

Name _____

Date _____ Period _____

Match the following terms and identifying statements. Terms may be used more than once.

_____ 1. Pastry cream to which whipped cream has been added.

_____ 2. Stable foam dessert that is solidified by fat or gelatin and lightened with whipped cream and sometimes Italian meringue.

_____ 3. Custard sauce that, in addition to being used as a sauce, is the base of important preparations such as Bavarian cream and many ice creams.

_____ 4. Foam made by beating egg whites with sugar.

_____ 5. Name of the process that gently raises the temperature of the egg yolks to prevent curdling.

_____ 6. A stable foam dessert made from crème anglaise that is bound with gelatin and lightened with whipped cream.

_____ 7. Sweetened milk that is thickened with starch and egg yolks.

_____ 8. Classical name for sweetened whipped cream.

_____ 9. The French word that means *foam*.

_____ 10. Its French name, commonly used in many kitchens, is *crème pâtissière*.

_____ 11. Is thickened solely by egg yolks, and must not be boiled during preparation.

A. Bavarian cream

B. crème anglaise

C. crème chantilly

D. crème mousseline

E. meringue

F. mousse

G. pastry cream

H. tempering

Various Forms of Custards and Foams

Chapter 42

Activity B

Name _____

Date _____ Period_____

Part 1: Custards

Circle the clue in parentheses that best completes each of the following statements.

1. Stirred custards are prepared (**in the oven**) (**on the stove top**).

2. Pastry cream is prepared (**in the oven**) (**on the stove top**).

3. Crème anglaise is prepared (**in the oven**) (**on the stove top**).

4. Pastry cream is also known as (**custard**) (**mousse**) (**crème mousseline**).

5. Pastry cream is sweetened milk thickened with (**starch and egg yolks**) (**starch**) (**egg yolks**) (**beaten egg whites**).

6. Pastry cream is considered a potentially hazardous food because it (**can be a breeding ground for pathogens**) (**it has a high fat content**).

7. Pastry cream is generally flavored with (**almond**) (**cinnamon**) (**vanilla**), but other flavors can be used as well.

8. Adding whipped cream to pastry cream creates (**crème anglaise**) (**crème mousseline**) (**Bavarian cream**).

9. Pastry cream has the consistency of (**thick pudding**) (**thick sauce**) (**thin sauce**).

10. In addition to its use as a sauce, (**crème anglaise**) (**mousse**) (**crème mousseline**) is the base of preparations such as Bavarian cream and many ice creams.

11. Crème anglaise is thickened solely by (**egg yolks**) (**starch**) (**gelatin**).

12. (**Pastry cream**) (**Crème anglaise**) must always be boiled.

13. (**Pastry cream**) (**Crème anglaise**) must never be boiled.

14. When preparing crème anglaise professional chefs know that the product is done when it is thick enough to coat the (**tines of a metal fork**) (**back of a wooden spoon**) or reaches a temperature between 180°F and 185°F (82°C and 85°C).

15. If crème anglaise (**gets too hot**) (**does not get hot enough**) the yolks do not thicken properly and the finished product is thin and watery.

16. If crème anglaise (**gets too hot**) (**does not get hot enough**) it will separate.

17. To help moderate the cooking process, (**baked custards**) (**stirred custards**) (**all custards**) are prepared in a bain marie.

(Continued)

Activity B *(Continued)*   Name _____

Part 2: Foams

Circle the clue in parentheses that best completes each of the following statements.

18. Whipped cream is lightened by (**egg whites**) (**gelatin**) (**air**).

19. Preferably, whipped cream is made from cream with a (**high**) (**medium**) (**low**) butterfat level.

20. One important rule when making whipped cream is to keep the cream (**cold**) (**warm**).

21. Most whipped cream is used between the (**very soft and soft**) (**soft and firm**) (**firm and stiff**) peak stages.

22. Adding sugar to whipped cream when the cream reaches the soft peak stage creates (**crème anglaise**) (**crème chantilly**) (**crème mousseline**).

23. Meringue is a foam made by beating (**egg whites**) (**egg yolks**) (**gelatin**) with sugar.

24. Overwhipping will destroy (**meringue**) (**whipped cream**) (**meringue and whipped cream**).

25. Properly made meringue is a(n) (**unstable**) (**stable**) foam.

26. Meringue made by combining all of the sugar and egg whites at once, cooking the mixture over boiling water, and then whipping it to firm peak stage is (**French meringue**) (**Swiss meringue**) (**Italian meringue**).

27. Meringue made by adding some of the sugar at the soft peak stage and then whipping the mixture to the firm peak stage, at which time the rest of the sugar is folded in is (**French meringue**) (**Swiss meringue**) (**Italian meringue**).

28. Meringue made by preparing a hot sugar and water syrup which is slowly poured into the egg whites as they are beaten at high speed is (**French meringue**) (**Swiss meringue**) (**Italian meringue**).

29. Two meringues that are generally piped into various shapes and baked at a low temperature are (**French and Swiss**) (**French and Italian**) (**Swiss and Italian**) meringue.

30. (**Mousse**) (**Bavarian cream**) (**Mousse and Bavarian cream**) is/are solidified by fat or gelatin and lightened with whipped cream and sometimes Italian meringue.

31. (**Mousse**) (**Bavarian cream**) (**Mousse and Bavarian cream**) is/are made from crème anglaise that is bound with gelatin and lightened with whipped cream.

32. (**Mousse**) (**Bavarian cream**) (**Mousse and Bavarian cream**) can be served alone or combined with other ingredients such as cake or fruit to make complex desserts.

Buttercreams

Chapter 42

Activity C

Name _____

Date _____ Period _____

Characteristics of buttercreams are listed in the left column of the chart below. Place a check (✓) in column that corresponds with the type of buttercream—American or French—being described. Some characteristics may require a check in both columns.

Comparison of Buttercreams		
	American	**French**
Consists of egg yolks, sugar syrup, and butter.		
Consists of softened butter and a large amount of powdered sugar.		
Is very sweet.		
Is less sweet.		
Is less stable in hot environments.		
Is very stable even in hot conditions.		
Is the preference of many pastry shops because it is the easiest to prepare.		
Is somewhat complicated to make.		
Is often referred to as frosting.		
Has a higher fat content.		
Can be flavored in many ways with the addition of extracts or melted chocolate.		
Once it is homogenous, it is ready to be used.		
If it is not used immediately, it should be refrigerated.		

Dessert Sauces and Frozen Desserts

Culinary Terminology

Chapter 43

Activity A

Name _____

Date _____ Period _____

Match the following terms and identifying statements. Terms may be used more than once.

_____ 1. Fruit sauces that are a mixture of puréed fruit, simple syrup, and, sometimes lemon juice.

_____ 2. A mixture made by combining chopped chocolate and boiling hot heavy cream.

_____ 3. This preparation should not be stirred as it cooks.

_____ 4. A slightly less-sweet style of sorbet.

_____ 5. A cross between sorbet and ice cream.

_____ 6. French name for a frozen mixture of fruit purée, sugar, and water.

_____ 7. Instrument that measures the sugar levels in fruit purées and syrups.

_____ 8. The name for the air that is frozen in ice cream.

_____ 9. Sugar that is cooked to about 320°F (160°C).

_____ 10. Adding high amounts of this to ice cream lowers the quality of the ice cream.

_____ 11. Once cooled, can be used for pastry specialties such as chocolate truffles and cake fillings and coverings.

_____ 12. The quality of this sauce is dependent on the quality of the fruit used.

_____ 13. A coulis-type mixture with the addition of a dairy product.

A. caramel

B. coulis

C. densimeter

D. ganache

E. granité

F. overrun

G. sherbet

H. sorbet

Preparing Dessert Sauces and Frozen Desserts

Chapter 43

Name _____

Activity B

Date _____Period_____

Circle the clue in parentheses that best completes each of the following statements.

1. One method of making chocolate sauce is to bring water, milk, or cream to a boil; add chopped chocolate; and then (**turn down**) (**turn up**) (**remove from**) heat. Stir until the chocolate has (**melted**) (**solidified**) and the sauce is homogenous.

2. The other method of making chocolate sauce is to melt chocolate in a (**granité**) (**densimeter**) (**baine marie**), add heated (**liquid**) (**sugar**), and stir until the desired consistency is reached.

3. Crème anglaise is considered a classic dessert sauce because it is of (**pourable**) (**spreadable**) consistency.

4. Step one of making caramel sauce is (**boiling the water**) (**cooking the sugar**).

5. When making caramel sauce, the sugar should (**always**) (**occasionally**) (**never**) be stirred.

6. Step two of making caramel sauce is adding liquid to the caramel to (**cool it down**) (**thin it out**) (**dilute the flavor**).

7. The liquid most often added when making caramel sauce is (**cold water**) (**hot water**) (**cold cream**) (**hot cream**) but could also be (**cold water**) (**hot water**) (**cold cream**) (**hot cream**).

8. Fruit sauces are the (**most difficult**) (**easiest**) sauces to make.

9. Fruit sauces are most often a mixture of puréed fruit, (**coulis**) (**powdered sugar**) (**simple syrup**), and lemon juice if needed.

10. If peaches and pears are not cooked before blending, they will (**be too hard**) (**turn brown**) (**spoil**).

11. Frozen fruit purées (**should never**) (**may be**) used as a substitute for fresh fruit in fruit sauces.

12. If a fruit sauce is too thick, (**water**) (**appropriate juice**) (**either water or appropriate juice**) is generally added to adjust the consistency.

13. Traditional ice cream begins with (**coulis**) (**ganache**) (**crème anglaise**).

(Continued)

Activity B *(Continued)*   **Name** _____

14. As the amount of butterfat in ice cream increases, the richness and quality of the ice cream (**increases**) (**decreases**).

15. Any ice cream product that is less than (**10**) (**20**) (**30**) percent butterfat must be labeled light, low fat, or reduced fat.

16. The purpose of continually churning ice cream as it freezes is to help (**form large ice crystals**) (**prevent the formation of large ice crystals**).

17. Air added to ice cream during mixing contributes to (**ice crystal formation**) (**a light texture**) (**a grainy texture**).

18. Ice creams that begin with crème anglaise are also called (**French**) (**eggless**) (**fruit**) ice creams.

19. Sorbet is most closely related to (**crème anglaise**) (**coulis**) (**ganache**).

20. The more sugar a sorbet contains, the (**softer**) (**harder**) the finished sorbet will be.

21. A granité is a style of sorbet that is often slightly (**more**) (**less**) sweet than regular sorbet.

22. Sherbet is a cross between (**ice cream and granité**) (**ice cream and sorbet**) (**granité and sorbet**).

Reviewing Key Concepts

Chapter 43

Activity C

Name _____

Date _____ Period _____

Read each statement below. Circle the letter *T* if the statement is true. If the statement is false, circle *F* and write the corrected statement on the lines that follow.

T   F   1.   Dessert sauces contribute flavor and moisture, as well as improve the appearance of a dessert.

_____

_____

T   F   2.   When adding cream to hot caramel, the cream should be added all at once.

_____

_____

T   F   3.   Once crème anglaise is cooled, it can be used to make truffles.

_____

_____

T   F   4.   Chocolate sauce shouldn't have flavors added because chocolate has a distinctive flavor.

_____

_____

T   F   5.   If the caramel browns irregularly when making caramel sauce, gently stir the sugar.

_____

_____

T   F   6.   If portions of a caramel sauce form lumps that do not dissolve, bring the mixture to a boil and stir until smooth.

_____

_____

T   F   7.   The quality of a coulis depends on the quantity of sugar.

_____

_____

(Continued)

Activity C (*Continued*)   **Name** _____

T F 8. *Overrun* is the name for air that is frozen in ice cream.

_____

_____

T F 9. Sorbet is a frozen mixture of fruit purée, sugar, and water.

_____

_____

T F 10. The amount of water in sorbet determines the texture of the finished sorbet.

_____

_____

T F 11. The proportion of water, puréed fruit, and sugar in sorbet is standard for all types of fruit sorbet.

_____

_____

T F 12. A granité is a coulis that is allowed to freeze in a shallow pan and is stirred from time to time as it freezes.

_____

_____

T F 13. Legally, sherbet must contain between 5 to 10 percent butterfat.

_____

_____

T F 14. Densimeters measure the moisture levels in fruit purées and syrups using the brix or baumé scales.

_____

_____

Notes

Food Presentation

Culinary Terminology

Name _____

Date _____Period_____

Match the following terms and identifying statements. Terms may be used more than once.

_____ 1. A balanced arrangement that is identical on opposite sides of a center point.

_____ 2. The point or item to which the eye is first drawn when looking at a plate presentation.

_____ 3. A decorative covered stand that keeps food hot.

_____ 4. Edible decorative addition or accompaniment to a dish.

_____ 5. A sense of balance achieved by artistically arranging items without creating two identical sides of a center point.

_____ 6. Enables chefs to serve hot foods at optimal temperatures at a buffet presentation.

_____ 7. Should improve appearance but never detract from the main dish.

_____ 8. Usually the highest, biggest, or most colorful item on the plate.

A. asymmetry

B. chafing dish

C. focal point

D. garnish

E. symmetry

Applying Presentation Principles

Chapter 44

Activity B

Name _____

Date _____Period_____

Part 1: Plating

Circle the clue in parentheses that best completes each of the following statements.

1. When planning plate presentation, foods that have (**similar**) (**contrasting**) colors look the most appetizing.

2. The plating process should happen rapidly to protect food (**balance**) (**temperature**).

3. Proportion refers to the relationship between the (**amounts**) (**textures**) (**colors**) of the different foods on a plate.

4. When planning a plate, chefs consider how the food (**covers the plate**) (**rises above the plate**) (**covers and rises above the plate**).

5. The focal point of a plate is usually (**the main item**) (**anything red**).

6. Repeating the same shapes on the plate should be (**a goal**) (**avoided**).

7. Overly tall food is likely to appear (**formal**) (**comical**).

8. Plate designs with a definite (**predominant color**) (**focal point**) create a satisfying sense of order.

9. Properly cooked foods usually (**have**) (**do not have**) naturally vibrant colors.

10. For balance, foods on a plate should have (**similar**) (**various**) textures.

11. (**Asymmetry**) (**Proportion**) (**Symmetry**) refers to the relationship between the size of the actual plate and the food arranged on it.

12. A plate cover is a device that helps chefs apply the (**focal point**) (**variety**) (**temperature**) plating principle.

13. Topping a mound of applesauce with a thin wedge of crisp fresh apple is an example of applying the plating principle of (**height**) (**color**) (**variety of texture**).

14. Serving a cold salad in a lukewarm bowl is an example of (**balancing temperature**) (**ignoring the plating principle of temperature**).

15. Color adds to a dish and a garnish may be used to improve the color of a plate (**regardless of its taste**) (**only if its taste complements the flavors of the dish**).

(Continued)

Activity B (*Continued*)   **Name** _____

Part 2: Platters and Buffets

Read each statement below. Circle the letter *T* if the statement is true. If the statement is false, circle *F* and write the corrected statement on the lines that follow.

T   F   16. On a platter, the focal point is often a centerpiece that is not meant to be eaten.

_____

_____

T   F   17. Platters with too much negative space appear crowded, those with too little appear empty.

_____

_____

T   F   18. A platter with identical sides split by a center point is an example of asymmetry.

_____

_____

T   F   19. If the food is to be served by a cook or server, portion sizes on a platter don't matter.

_____

_____

T   F   20. The same considerations that pertain to a platter pertain to an entire buffet.

_____

_____

T   F   21. Buffets are always arranged symmetrically.

_____

_____

T   F   22. Two aspects of functionality related to buffet design to consider are keeping the buffet clean and well stocked.

_____

_____

(Continued)

Activity B (*Continued*)   **Name** _____

T   F   23. Buffet centerpieces are similar to platter centerpieces but generally smaller.

_____

_____

T   F   24. Chafing dishes are often used in buffets to keep cold foods cold.

_____

_____

Garnishing Techniques

Chapter 44

Activity C

Name _____

Date _____ Period_____

Part 1

Circle the clue in parentheses that best completes each of the following statements.

1. Garnishes should (**coordinate**) (**contrast**) with the flavors and temperature of the dish.

2. Garnishes (**may**) (**should not**) overshadow the main dish.

3. Garnishes should be used (**only if functional**) (**even if only for visual stimulus**).

4. Herbs suitable for garnishing hot foods include (**cilantro, chervil, and basil**) (**thyme, rosemary, and parsley**).

5. When making a scallion flower, make as many (**horizontal**) (**lengthwise**) cuts down the scallion as possible. Roll the scallion (**45°**) (**90°**) and cut a new series of slices. Place the scallion in (**hot**) (**warm**) (**cool**) (**ice**) water for 30 minutes.

6. When making a radish rose, begin cutting when the radish is (**cold**) (**at room temperature**). Start at the (**top**) (**bottom**) of the radish, and cut petals on the sides of the radish. Petals should be about (**1/16-inch**) (**1/8-inch**) (**1/4-inch**) thick.

7. When making a tomato rose, you create the petals of the rose from a strip of the tomato (**pulp**) (**skin**). When formed, tomato roses should be stored in (**cold water**) (**the refrigerator**). Make tomato roses (**as far ahead**) (**as close to service**) as possible.

(Continued)

Activity C *(Continued)*   **Name** _____

Part 2

Answer the following in the space provided.

8. List four examples of crispy garnishes.

    _____

    _____

    _____

    _____

9. In addition to contributing a crunch to the eating experience, crispy items add height
    and a sense of _____ to the plate.

10. What type of vegetables are good choices for making vegetable cutouts? _____

    List three. _____

    _____

    _____

Table Service

45

Culinary Terminology

Chapter 45

Activity A

Name _____

Date _____ Period _____

Match the following terms and identifying statements.

_____ 1. Style of service in which the server delivers plates of food directly from the kitchen to the guest.

_____ 2. Style of service in which the waitperson places platters of prepared food in the center of the table and guests serve themselves.

_____ 3. A computer-based ordering system that transmits the order to the kitchen, produces the customer's bill, and keeps track of important data.

_____ 4. Style of service in which servers prepare dishes in front of the guests.

_____ 5. Dining room manager responsible for the entire dining room operations.

_____ 6. Style of service in which the front-of-house staff serves food from a platter onto preset plates in front of the guests.

_____ 7. Kitchen personnel.

_____ 8. Includes the china, flatware, glassware, and napkin used by one person.

_____ 9. The name for knives, forks, and spoons.

_____ 10. A tool used to scrape and scoop crumbs from the table.

_____ 11. Service personnel that work the dining room.

_____ 12. Refers to a dish that a server finishes by setting it aflame at tableside.

A. American service

B. back-of-the-house staff

C. crumber

D. family-style service

E. flambé

F. flatware

G. French service

H. front-of-the-house staff

I. maître d'hôtel

J. place setting

K. point-of-sale (POS) system

L. Russian service

The Front-of-the-House Staff

Chapter 45

Activity B

Name _____

Date _____ Period _____

Part 1: Positions

Match the positions with their descriptions of duties.

_____ 1. Principally responsible for clearing dirty dishes, changing linens, and resetting tables. Is also responsible for butter, bread, and water service.

_____ 2. Sometimes called *captain*. Welcomes guests, presents menus, takes orders, serves the food, provides beverage service, and is responsible for the bill. They must coordinate the needs of the guests with other front-of-the-house positions as well as the kitchen staff.

_____ 3. Responsible for taking reservations and booking parties via the telephone and the Internet.

_____ 4. Aids the front server and is responsible for coordinating timing with the chef and delivering food from the kitchen to the dining room.

_____ 5. Welcomes the guests to the dining room and, in many restaurants, leads the guests to their table and manages the reservations.

_____ 6. Is responsible for the entire dining room operation. This position is to the dining room what the chef is to the kitchen.

A. back server

B. busperson

C. front server

D. host

E. maître d'hôtel

F. reservationist

Part 2: Keys to Quality Service

For each key to quality service below, select the statement that is the best example of that skill and write the letter in the blank provided.

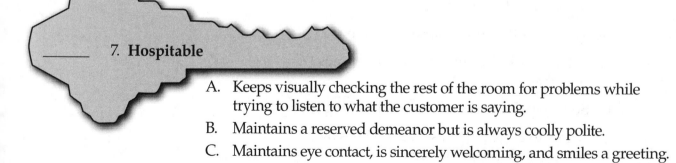

_____ 7. **Hospitable**

    A. Keeps visually checking the rest of the room for problems while trying to listen to what the customer is saying.

    B. Maintains a reserved demeanor but is always coolly polite.

    C. Maintains eye contact, is sincerely welcoming, and smiles a greeting.

(Continued)

Activity B (*Continued*)   **Name** _____

_____ 8. **Poised**

    A. Helps the customers realize that they are not the only guests in the restaurant.

    B. Has developed strategies for staying calm and confident even when problems arise.

    C. Protects the front-of-the-house staff reputation by making sure that the guests are aware when problems are the fault of the back-of-the house staff.

_____ 9. **Knowledgeable**

    A. Is willing to take a guess at answering customers' questions, especially when the house is busy.

    B. Honestly tells the guests that they just don't know the answer to a question, if that is the case.

    C. Takes time to learn as much as possible about the food being served that day.

_____ 10. **Sense of Timing**

    A. Stays focused on what is happening in the dining room at all times, anticipates customer needs, and does a good job of prioritizing tasks.

    B. Brings food promptly, whenever the kitchen has it ready.

    C. Tries to coordinate two tables so that the job of serving both is easier.

(Continued)

Activity B *(Continued)*   **Name** _____

_____ 11. **Communication Skills**

        A. Anticipates customer questions and saves time by cutting in when he or she has the idea.

        B. Uses nonverbal cues to let the customer know he or she is listening. Always allows the customer to finish what he or she has to say before responding.

        C. Helps customers get to the point by showing that he or she is busy through body language and expression.

_____ 12. **Ability to "Read" the Customer**

        A. Carefully considers verbal and nonverbal cues to determine how the customer wants to be treated by the server.

        B. Treats all people alike regardless of their social status.

        C. Honestly shows their own personality, whether it is formal or folksy, and consistently treats all guests according to that style. Takes time to help customers adjust to that style with humor when possible.

Reviewing Key Concepts

Chapter 45

Activity C

Name _____

Date _____ Period _____

Part 1: Meal Service Styles

The four main styles of meal service are *American, family-style, French*, and *Russian*. Write the style of meal service that best matches each description.

Description   **Style of Meal Service**

1. An informal style of service common in restaurants and banquet halls across America.   _____

2. Requires that the servers cook and prepare dishes in front of the customer.   _____

3. The server delivers plates of food directly from the kitchen to the guest.   _____

4. The server must learn to hold a large fork and spoon in their dominant hand and use them like a pair of tongs to serve food.   _____

5. Food is served by front-of-the-house staff from a platter onto preset plates in front of guests.   _____

6. Often called *tableside service*.   _____

7. Is the norm in American restaurants and can be a formal or informal service style depending on the restaurant.   _____

8. Waitperson places platters of prepared food on the table and guests serve themselves.   _____

Part 2: Presetting the Dining Area

Circle the clue in parentheses that best completes each of the following statements.

9. When just prior to serving each course, the appropriate flatware and glassware are placed in front of each guest, the place setting is (**basic American**) (**à la carte**) (**banquet**).

10. A service that consists of a dinner plate, one or two forks, spoon, knife, water glass, any additional glassware, a butter knife, and bread and butter plate is (**basic American**) (**à la carte**) (**banquet**).

11. A setting that has all needed glassware and flatware on the table before people are seated is (**basic American**) (**à la carte**) (**banquet**).

(Continued)

Activity C *(Continued)*   **Name** _____

Part 3: Serving Guests

Read each statement below. Circle the letter *T* if the statement is true. If the statement is false, circle *F* and write the corrected statement on the lines that follow.

T   F   12. When pouring water in front of the guest, pour from the left of the customer.

_____

_____

T   F   13. One clue that indicates the table is ready to order is when most guests have set their menus back on the table after looking at them.

_____

_____

T   F   14. Plates of food are always transported from the kitchen to the dining room on a rolling cart pushed by the server.

_____

_____

T   F   15. Once the food is served, the back servers are relieved of their responsibility.

_____

_____

T   F   16. About mid-meal, the front server should ask the customer if everything is to the customer's liking.

_____

_____

T   F   17. If the host is not known, the server should guess who the host is and present that person with the check.

_____

_____

(Continued)

Activity C *(Continued)*   **Name** _____

Part 4: Beverages

T   F   18. Espresso is a combination of cappuccino and steamed milk.

_____

_____

T   F   19. Cappuccino is a combination of espresso, steamed milk, and milk foam.

_____

_____

T   F   20. The finest teas are sold in bags.

_____

_____

T   F   21. If using tea bags, the customer is brought the tea and a small pot of warm water.

_____

_____

Notes

Culinary Terminology

Chapter 46

Activity A

Name _____

Date _____ Period _____

Match the following terms and identifying statements.

_____ 1. A person who knows and can discuss your work history and personal qualities.

_____ 2. Opportunity to receive instruction on specific skills or procedures of the job while working.

_____ 3. Any unwelcome sexual advance, request for sexual favor, and other verbal or physical conduct of a sexual nature that affects a person's ability to work.

_____ 4. A formal business letter that introduces a candidate to a potential employer.

_____ 5. Act passed in 1938 to protect workers from unfair treatment by employers.

_____ 6. Refers to valuing and respecting the contributions of coworkers who are different from you.

_____ 7. Non-wage, financial extras provided by employers to their employees.

_____ 8. How you feel about your job and how much effort you put into it.

_____ 9. US agency responsible for the oversight and coordination of all federal equal opportunity regulations, practices, and policies.

_____ 10. A summary of the important information about an applicant.

_____ 11. The lowest hourly rate of pay that an employee can be paid legally.

_____ 12. A length of time during which the supervisor observes a new employee to see if he or she is able to perform the job.

_____ 13. A method for dealing with unacceptable job-related behavior in a step process.

A. benefits

B. cover letter

C. Equal Employment Opportunity Commission (EEOC)

D. Fair Labor Standards Act (FLSA)

E. minimum wage

F. on-the-job training

G. probation period

H. progressive discipline

I. reference

J. résumé

K. sexual harassment

L. work ethic

M. workplace diversity

Reviewing Key Concepts

Chapter 46

Activity B

Name _____

Date _____ Period_____

Part 1: The Search for Job Opportunities

Circle the clue in parentheses that best completes each of the following statements.

1. When trying to identify an appropriate job, you should take an honest assessment of the skill level (**to which you aspire**) (**you presently have**).

2. A parent or other relative (**can**) (**cannot**) be a job-search contact.

3. An acceptable reference is your (**coach**) (**relative**) (**coach or relative**).

4. A good résumé is (**long and detailed**) (**short and concise**).

5. You should find three adults that agree to serve as references (**when you are asked for references at an interview**) (**before beginning your job search**).

6. A work history (**should**) (**should not**) include internships and volunteer positions.

7. Mentioning awards, licenses, and certificates on a résumé is (**appropriate**) (**not appropriate**).

8. You (**should**) (**should not**) list languages spoken on your résumé.

9. Communicating with your job-search contacts to let them know you are looking for a job is called (**work ethic**) (**networking**).

10. List four possible sources of information on job opportunities that you could use to find jobs.

_____

_____

Part 2: Submitting Your Résumé

Read each statement below. Circle the letter *T* if the statement is true. If the statement is false, circle *F* and write the corrected statement on the lines that follow.

T   F   11. Once you identify a job opportunity, you should submit your résumé promptly.

_____

_____

(Continued)

Activity B (*Continued*)   Name _____

T F 12. Although some companies give directions for the preferred format for a résumé, a generic format is always acceptable.

_____

_____

T F 13. A résumé that is used on the Internet is usually referred to as a computer résumé.

_____

_____

T F 14. Cover letters are always optional.

_____

_____

T F 15. A good cover letter is long, detailed, and provides full background, as well as your future plans and desires.

_____

_____

Part 3: The Job Application

Circle the clue in parentheses that best completes each of the following statements.

16. It is (**important**) (**unnecessary**) to bring more information than your résumé when applying for a job because job applications (**often**) (**rarely**) request additional information.

17. Hiring managers typically review the prospective employee's (**résumé rather than job application**) (**job application rather than résumé**) (**résumé and job application**).

18. When filling out a job application, neatness (**is**) (**is not**) important.

19. Questions left unanswered (**are not important**) (**raise concerns**).

20. Your answers to questions on a job application (**must match**) (**typically vary slightly from**) the information given on your résumé.

Reviewing Key Concepts

Chapter 46   Name _____

Activity C   Date _____Period_____

Part 1: Effective Job Interviews

Complete the following statements describing ways to be effective during the job interview.

1. Prepare for the interview by _____

   _____ .

2. Dress appropriately by looking _____

   _____ .

3. Introduce yourself with a smile and _____

   _____ .

4. Answer the interviewer's questions_____

   _____ .

5. Ask questions that are _____

   _____ .

Part 2: Expectations

6. List five expectations that employers have of their employees.

   _____

   _____

   _____

   _____

   _____

7. List five things that employees can expect their employer to provide.

   _____

   _____

   _____

   _____

   _____

(Continued)

Activity C *(Continued)*   **Name** _____

Part 3: Laws of Employment

Circle the clue in parentheses that best completes each of the following statements.

8. There are local, state, and federal laws that (**employers**) (**employees**) (**employers and employees**) must follow.

9. The (**FLSA**) (**EEOC**) establishes minimum wage, overtime pay, and child labor standards.

10. Employers (**may not be**) (**are always**) required to pay minimum wage to all employees.

11. The employer must pay at least (**1 ½**) (**2**) times the employee's regular rate of pay for all hours worked over (**35**) (**40**) in a work week.

12. The FLSA does not limit the number of hours in a day or the number of days in a week that an employer may require an employee to work as long as the employee is at least (**16**) (**18**) (**21**) years old.

13. State laws (**may be**) (**cannot be**) stricter than the FLSA regulations.

14. The (**FLSA**) (**EEOC**) is responsible for the oversight and coordination of all federal equal employment opportunity regulations, practices, and policies.

15. Title VII of the Civil Rights Act of 1964 makes it illegal to discriminate against anyone because of race, color, sex, and (**national origin**) (**religion**) (**national origin or religion**).

16. A company (**may**) (**may not**) require a preemployment drug screening.

17. A company (**may**) (**may not**) require a criminal background check.

18. A company (**may**) (**may not**) require a credit history check.

19. A company (**may**) (**may not**) require verification of degrees and work experience.

20. A company (**may**) (**may not**) require employment eligibility verification.

21. A company (**may**) (**may not**) require employees to be a minimum age.

Notes

Culinary History

Culinary Terminology

Name _____

Date _____ Period _____

Complete the following statements about culinary history. Then arrange the circled letters to solve problem 7.

1. The highest level of the culinary arts in which the most challenging dishes are prepared is __ O __ O __ __ __ __ __ __ __ O

2. An area's __ __ __ __ __ O __ __ O __ O __ __ __ __ are native or traditional to that particular geographic region or ethnic population.

3. O __ __ __ __ __ __ __ O __ __ __ __ merges two or more ethnic cooking styles into one.

4. A style of cooking that highlighted individual ingredients that were simply prepared and served in small portions on artistic plates is __ O __ __ __ __ __ __ O __ __ O __ __ __.

5. Escoffier developed __ __ __ O __ __ __ __ __ __ __ __ __ O which used orderly menus organized by courses that were served tableside by waiters.

6. Popular in the early 1800s, O O __ __ __ __ __ O __ __ __ __ __ was an elaborate and time-consuming style of cooking that was often practiced in the homes of the rich.

Circled letters: _____

7. One of the most revered chefs, __ __ __ __ __ __ __ __ __ __ __ __ __ __ __ stressed that cooks and chefs should always act as professionally as possible so that they would be respected as professionals.

Influences on Culinary Practices

Chapter 47

Activity B

Name _____

Date _____ Period _____

Match the following time periods with the descriptions of developments in culinary practices. Time periods may be used more than once.

_____ 1. During this period, the Arabs invaded various lands and ruled for hundreds of years. With the invasion of Arabian culture came new cooking techniques and ingredients including almonds, eggplant, citrus fruits, spices, sugar, and rice. Arabs introduced distillation and the addition of sugar and ground nuts to many savory preparations.

_____ 2. Diets of this era were very different for various classes. While most of the population existed on simple foods prepared in simple ways, the wealthy ate a variety of foods prepared in very complex ways. The chefs of the wealthy were exposed to and learned to use costly imported items such as spices, hams, and oysters.

_____ 3. The French Revolution caused many chefs who worked in private homes to find themselves without jobs. Necessity gave them a new idea. They opened restaurants. Notably, Antonin Carême wrote books in which he refined and systemized the grande cuisine.

_____ 4. The first complete Western cookbook was written during this time and was subsequently revised over the next several hundred years. It described challenging culinary dishes with complex flavor profiles and remained the most important cookbook for some time.

_____ 5. People in this era focused on food products rather than on elaborate cooking techniques. Cooking techniques centered on spit roasting, boiling, baking, and grilling. Foods included olives, honey, cheese, seafood, grain, lamb, and wild herbs.

_____ 6. A time of rapid technological change. Foods from other countries became readily available and new inventions, such as the microwave, food processor, and convection ovens, changed the way commercial kitchens operated.

A. 1700s and 1800s

B. 1900s

C. Ancient Egypt

D. Ancient Greece

E. Ancient Rome

F. Middle Ages

G. Renaissance

(Continued)

Activity B *(Continued)*   **Name** _____

_____ 7. People of this era made yeast-raised and flat breads, tended bees, domesticated animals for milk and meat, and cooked fish.

_____ 8. During this period, the first voyages to the Americas introduced new products such as tomatoes, potatoes, peppers, corn, and chocolate to Europe.

_____ 9. During this era, the Catholic Church, through the efforts of its monasteries, preserved records of ancient cooking practices and preserved and improved the art of baking as well as techniques for making cheese, wine, and beer.

_____ 10. During this period, the marriage of Caterina de Medici to King Henry II of France contributed to the slow and steady refining of French cooking that would lead to the popularity of French cuisine around the world in the centuries that followed.

A. 1700s and 1800s

B. 1900s

C. Ancient Egypt

D. Ancient Greece

E. Ancient Rome

F. Middle Ages

G. Renaissance

Reviewing Key Concepts

Chapter 47

Activity C

Name _____

Date _____ Period _____

Part 1

Read each statement below. Circle the letter *T* if the statement is true. If the statement is false, circle *F* and write the corrected statement on the lines that follow.

T   F   1.   The knowledge chefs learn by studying culinary history gives them a better understanding of the present state of cuisine and where it is headed in the future.

_____

_____

T   F   2.   The development of agriculture improved standards of living for ancient cultures and resulted in more complex cooking practices.

_____

_____

T   F   3.   Grande cuisine, refined and systemized in the 1800s, was based on serving simple foods that were simply prepared.

_____

_____

T   F   4.   Many of the chefs who introduced nouvelle cuisine were influenced by French food traditions.

_____

_____

T   F   5.   Escoffier simplified grande cuisine by serving fewer, less complicated dishes to create classic cuisine.

_____

_____

(Continued)

Activity C (*Continued*)   **Name** _____

T F 6. The highest level of the culinary arts where the most challenging dishes are prepared is fusion cuisine.

_____

_____

T F 7. Air travel allowed easy contact between chefs in various countries, which has influenced cuisine development.

_____

_____

Part 2

Complete the flowchart below, which shows the progression of styles of cuisine in sequence by writing one of the following terms in the spaces provided: *Classic, Fusion, Grande, Nouvelle.*

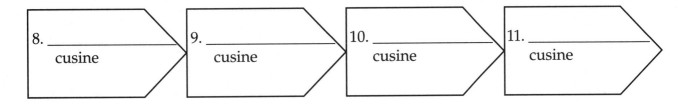

8. _____ cusine

9. _____ cusine

10. _____ cusine

11. _____ cusine

Part 3

Complete the following in the space provided.

12. The television chef star who popularized French cooking in the United States beginning in the 1960s is _____ .

13. Name four types of ethnic cuisines other than French that chefs introduced to the American palate beginning in the 1980s.

_____   _____

_____   _____

14. Chefs that mixed different ethnic cuisines to create a new type of cuisine called it _____ cuisine.

(Continued)

Activity C *(Continued)*   **Name** _____

15. While some chefs were exploring ethnic cuisines, others were creating variations of
    traditional regional favorites. Name one example of such a dish.

    _____

16. Explain the term *melting pot cuisine* in relationship to the United States.

    _____

    _____

    _____

    _____

    _____

    _____

    _____

Nutrition

Culinary Terminology

Chapter 48

Activity A

Name _____

Date _____Period_____

Part 1

Match the following terms and identifying statements.

_____ 1. Foods that have high nutritional value compared with the amount of calories they supply.

_____ 2. Chief energy source for the body.

_____ 3. Are missing one or more of the nine indispensable amino acids.

_____ 4. The way our body takes in and utilizes foods.

_____ 5. Unit used to measure the amount of energy contained in foods.

_____ 6. Nutrients that the body cannot make, and therefore must be supplied by diet.

_____ 7. Substances in food that nourish the body.

_____ 8. Contain all nine indispensable amino acids in the correct proportions needed to support life.

_____ 9. Type of lipid that is created when unsaturated oil is chemically changed to resemble a saturated fat.

A. calorie

B. carbohydrate

C. complete protein

D. essential nutrients

E. incomplete protein

F. nutrient-dense food

G. nutrients

H. nutrition

I. *trans* fat

(Continued)

Activity A (*Continued*)   **Name** _____

Part 2

_____ 10. Consists of three fatty acids that are linked together by a glycerol molecule.

_____ 11. White, pasty substance found in the bloodstream and cells that is essential for many body functions.

_____ 12. A set of recommended values for nutrient intakes for healthy individuals and defined groups.

_____ 13. The scientific term for fat.

_____ 14. A molecule made up of a chain of various amino acids linked together in a particular order.

_____ 15. Chemical process that changes liquid oil into solid fat.

_____ 16. A food guidance system that helps people select the right foods in the right amounts to meet their individual needs.

A. cholesterol

B. dietary reference intakes (DRI)

C. hydrogenation

D. lipid

E. MyPyramid

F. protein

G. triglyceride

The Role of Nutrients in Good Health

Chapter 48

Activity B

Name _____

Date _____Period_____

Circle the clue in parentheses that best completes each of the following statements.

1. The most energy-dense nutrient that humans consume is (**vitamins**) (**minerals**) (**protein**) (**lipids**) (**water**) (**carbohydrates**).

2. The nutrient that accounts for 50 to 60 percent of the weight of the human body is (**vitamins**) (**minerals**) (**protein**) (**lipids**) (**water**) (**carbohydrates**).

3. The nutrient that is referred to as the building blocks of the human body is (**vitamins**) (**minerals**) (**protein**) (**lipids**) (**water**) (**carbohydrates**).

4. The nutrient that ensures proper vision, supports the immune system, aids in the formation of healthy bones and teeth, and is part of the blood clotting process is (**vitamins**) (**minerals**) (**protein**) (**lipids**) (**water**) (**carbohydrates**).

5. The nutrient that is the body's chief energy source is (**vitamins**) (**minerals**) (**protein**) (**lipids**) (**water**) (**carbohydrates**).

6. The nutrient that is necessary for energy metabolism, bone formation, and proper functioning of the nervous system is (**vitamins**) (**minerals**) (**protein**) (**lipids**) (**water**) (**carbohydrates**).

7. The nutrient that is further classified as either fat soluble or water soluble is (**vitamins**) (**minerals**) (**protein**) (**lipids**) (**water**) (**carbohydrates**).

8. The nutrient that is part of skin, blood vessels, blood, inner organs, hair, nails, and enzymes is (**vitamins**) (**minerals**) (**protein**) (**lipids**) (**water**) (**carbohydrates**).

9. Linoleic and linolenic acids are essential fatty acids that are part of the (**vitamins**) (**minerals**) (**protein**) (**lipids**) (**water**) (**carbohydrates**) nutrient group.

10. The nutrient that provides no energy but is part of almost all bodily functions is (**vitamins**) (**minerals**) (**protein**) (**lipids**) (**water**) (**carbohydrates**).

11. The nutrient that is further divided into major or trace categories is (**vitamins**) (**minerals**) (**protein**) (**lipids**) (**water**) (**carbohydrates**).

12. Fiber, which helps protect against some cancers, is part of the (**vitamins**) (**minerals**) (**protein**) (**lipids**) (**water**) (**carbohydrates**) group of nutrients.

Dietary Guidelines

Chapter 48

Activity C

Name _____

Date _____ Period_____

Answer the following.

1. Summarize the three basic messages around which the *Dietary Guidelines for Americans* provide advice. _____

   _____

   _____

   _____

2. Why should most of your fruit choices be whole or cut-up fruit rather than juice?

   _____

3. What portion of the grains eaten should be whole grain?

   _____

4. What should you look for when choosing a protein source to meet your needs?

   _____

   _____

5. The *Guidelines* recommend being physically active for at least how long every day? _____. Children and teenagers should be active for how long every day? _____.

6. The number of calories your body needs depends on whether you are trying to gain, maintain, or lose weight along with what five personal factors? _____

   _____

   _____

7. What specifically does the MyPyramid food guidance system help people select when choosing foods?_____

   _____

8. MyPyramid divides commonly eaten foods into oils and what five groups? _____

   _____

   _____

(Continued)

Activity C *(Continued)*   **Name** _____

9. In addition to designing personalized food plans and personal nutritional analysis, what
    are four other types of information offered on the MyPyramid Web site?_____

    _____

    _____

    _____

    _____

10. What age range does the MyPyramid Web site serve? _____

    _____

Labeling and the Chef's Role

Chapter 48   Name _____

Activity D   Date _____Period_____

Part 1

Circle either *required* or *voluntary* to indicate whether each of the following items is required for ingredient labeling of foods.

required   *voluntary*   1. A list of all ingredients in the product.

required   *voluntary*   2. Ingredients listed in descending order by weight.

required   *voluntary*   3. Content of each ingredient as a percentage of the whole.

required   *voluntary*   4. Flavorings listed by their common names.

required   *voluntary*   5. The name of the food source of any major food allergens contained in the product.

Part 2

Circle the clue in parentheses that best completes each of the following statements.

6. The first item on a nutrition label is (**amount of fat**) (**number of calories**) (**serving size**).

7. All the nutritional information listed on the Nutrition Facts panel is based on (**one serving**) (**two servings**) (**servings for a family of four**).

8. To the right of each nutrient listed on a Nutrition Facts panel is the percent Daily Values for all the nutrients except *trans* fat, sugar, and (**cholesterol**) (**sodium**) (**protein**).

9. The percent Daily Value is based on a (**1200-**) (**2000-**) (**2500-**) calorie diet.

10. The chef's role in promoting healthy eating is (**increasing**) (**staying the same**) (**decreasing**).

11. One way chefs influence the nutrition of diners is by choosing nutrient-dense foods, which are foods that (**are heavy by weight**) (**contain a variety of nutrients**) (**have high nutritional value for each calorie**).

12. Substituting healthy oils for saturated fats, steaming vegetables instead of boiling them, and trimming excess fats from meats are examples of the way that chefs influence the nutrition of diners by (**using healthy cooking techniques**) (**cutting calories**).

13. Restaurants typically (**do**) (**do not**) serve healthy ratios of protein to grains and vegetables.

14. Portion sizes in restaurants are typically (**too large**) (**too small**) (**just right**) because chefs are caught between the nutritional goal of (**smaller**) (**larger**) portions and the customers desire for value.

Managing Resources

Culinary Terminology

Chapter 49

Activity A

Name _____

Date _____ Period _____

Part 1

Match the following terms and identifying statements.

_____ 1. A specific amount of product to be kept on hand in order to maintain a sufficient supply from one delivery to the next.

_____ 2. A document listing the items, quantities ordered, and the agreed prices.

_____ 3. Refers to the amount of food product that remains after cleaning, cooking, or other preparation.

_____ 4. A list of the quantities of products and their prices that are being delivered.

_____ 5. What results when a business' expenses are greater than its sales.

_____ 6. The dollars received by a foodservice operation in payment for a meal.

_____ 7. Indicates the raw, unprepared product in the same form it is delivered from the vendor.

_____ 8. The cost of food used to make a menu item for a customer.

_____ 9. A business report that lists the sales and expenses incurred to make those sales during a given period of time.

A. as purchased (AP)

B. edible portion (EP)

C. food cost

D. invoice

E. loss

F. par stock

G. profit and loss statement (P&L)

H. purchase order (PO)

I. sales

(Continued)

Copyright by Goodheart-Willcox Co., Inc.

Activity A *(Continued)*   **Name** _____

Part 2

_____ 10. Includes all the expenses involved in maintaining a foodservice staff.

_____ 11. The process of determining and recording the usable amount, or edible portion, of a product.

_____ 12. What results when a business' sales are greater than its expenses.

_____ 13. The costs incurred to prepare and serve the meal.

_____ 14. Predicting how many diners will be served during the coming meal period and what menu items they will order.

_____ 15. The ratio of EP to AP.

_____ 16. The portion of food sales that was spent on food expenses.

A. expenses

B. food cost percentage

C. forecast

D. labor cost

E. profit

F. yield percentage

G. yield test

Managing Costs

Chapter 49

Activity B

Name _____

Date _____Period_____

Part 1: Food Costs

Read each statement below. Circle the letter *T* if the statement is true. If the statement is false, circle *F* and write the corrected statement on the lines that follow.

T   F   1.   The goal of purchasing is to assure that the kitchen gets the right product at the right price in the right quantity.

_____

_____

T   F   2.   An inventory is taken by estimating the amounts of various food products in house.

_____

_____

T   F   3.   The prices of food products are generally stable and seldom change.

_____

_____

T   F   4.   Procedures for receiving food products are a matter of inspection and paying.

_____

_____

T   F   5.   Shelf space is the key to product shelf life.

_____

_____

T   F   6.   Product rotation ensures that the most recently purchased items are used first.

_____

_____

(Continued)

Activity B (*Continued*)   **Name** _____

T   F   7.   Theft of food products is most often committed by a restaurant's customers.

_____

_____

T   F   8.   Before cooks can begin their mise en place, the chef must forecast how many diners will be served during the coming meal period and what will be ordered.

_____

_____

T   F   9.   Chef's base their forecasts on past business statistics.

_____

_____

T   F   10. The chef uses a profit and loss sheet to communicate the number of each menu item the staff should prepare for meal service.

_____

_____

T   F   11. One reason to cost out a recipe is to aid in accurate menu pricing.

_____

_____

T   F   12. Yield tests are done most frequently on the least expensive ingredients in the kitchen.

_____

_____

T   F   13. A yield test is the ratio of EP to AP.

_____

_____

(Continued)

Activity B *(Continued)*   **Name** _____

Part 2: Labor Costs

Circle the clue in parentheses that best completes each of the following statements.

14. The most important tool in controlling (**overall**) (**labor**) (**food waste**) costs is the staff schedule.

15. Most operations schedule kitchen staff on a (**daily**) (**weekly**) (**monthly**) basis.

16. Before creating the schedule, the chef needs to forecast the expected (**volume of business**) (**cost of sales**) for the week.

17. The largest cost in most foodservice operations is (**food**) (**labor**).

18. The actual labor cost is kept in check best by (**enforcing**) (**overlooking**) rules regarding the time clock or time sheets.

19. If the amount of business forecasted doesn't materialize, chefs (**must accept the loss**) (**may adjust the staff schedule**).

20. All decisions in scheduling and pay rates must be in accordance with (**federal**) (**state**) (**federal and state**) laws.

Calculating Food Cost Percentage

Chapter 49

Activity C

Name _____

Date _____ Period_____

Part 1

Food cost percentage shows the portion of food sales that was spent on food expenses. It is an important measure of how well a chef is managing the kitchen operation. Use the following formula to solve the problems below. Show your work in the space provided.

Food costs ÷ Food sales = Food cost percentage

Example: During the month of May, ABC restaurant spent $43,600 on food to prepare menu items, which generated $119,900 in food sales. Use the formula to calculate ABC restaurant's food cost percentage.

Food costs ÷ Food sales = [quotient as a decimal] x 100 = Food cost percentage

$43,600 ÷ $119,900 = 0.3636 x 100 = 36.36% (round up to 36.4%)

1. A restaurant had food costs of $28,300 and food sales of $61,000 during January. What was their food cost percentage? _____%

2. A restaurant had food costs of $34,400 and food sales of $72,500 during March. What was their food cost percentage for March? _____%

3. In April, the restaurant in Problem 2 experienced a change. Food costs stayed the same, but food sales increased to $81,200. What was their food cost percentage for April? _____%

(Continued)

Activity C *(Continued)*   **Name** _____

4. Suppose that food costs for the restaurant in Problem 2 stayed the same in April, but sales decreased to $69,500. What would their food cost percentage be for April? _____%

5. Suppose instead that food costs for the restaurant in Problem 2 decreased in April to $32, 900 and sales stayed the same as in March. What would their food cost percentage be for April? _____%

6. If the restaurant in Problem 2 experienced an increase in food costs to $36,700 in April and food sales stayed the same as in March, what would their food cost percentage be for April? _____%

Part 2

Circle the clue in parentheses that best completes each of the following statements.

7. If food costs stay constant and sales increase, food cost percentage (**increases**) (**stays the same**) (**decreases**).

8. If food costs stay constant and sales decrease, food cost percentage (**increases**) (**stays the same**) (**decreases**).

9. If food costs decrease and sales stay constant, food cost percentage (**increases**) (**stays the same**) (**decreases**).

10. If food costs increase and sales stay constant, food cost percentage (**increases**) (**stays the same**) (**decreases**).

Notes

Menus

Culinary Terminology

Chapter 50

Activity A

Name _____

Date _____ Period_____

Match the following terms and descriptive statements. Terms may be used more than once.

_____ 1. Menu format that rotates a set number of items over a certain period of time. After that time period, the daily menu offerings repeat.

_____ 2. Menu format that has one set price for the total meal but allows customers to make their own selection from each course offered.

_____ 3. Menu format that offers one set meal to all guests with no choices or substitutions.

_____ 4. Menu format composed daily based on what food products are available in the market that day.

_____ 5. Menu format that prices each course separately.

_____ 6. Menu format that offers the same items every day.

_____ 7. Today, a banquet is the most common use of this menu format.

_____ 8. A modified form of this menu format used in the United States prices each main course separately, but that price includes other courses such as soup or salad and accompaniments.

_____ 9. This menu format is most often found in fine-dining establishments.

_____ 10. This menu format allows chefs to use the best products available at any given time.

_____ 11. This menu format is effective in operations that serve the same customers day after day, such as schools and hospitals.

_____ 12. One disadvantage of this menu format is that repeat customers might become bored with the unchanging menu offerings.

A. à la carte menu

B. cycle menu

C. market menu

D. prix fixe menu

E. static menu

F. table d'hôte menu

Menu Planning

Chapter 50

Activity B

Name _____

Date _____ Period _____

Read each statement below. Circle the letter *T* if the statement is true. If the statement is false, circle *F* and write the corrected statement on the lines that follow.

T   F   1.   The goal of good menu planning is to create a mix of menu items that satisfies diners at the lowest possible price.

_____

_____

T   F   2.   The term *menu mix* refers to mixing the menu formats in a restaurant.

_____

_____

T   F   3.   In addition to pleasing the customers, it is important to choose a combination of menu items that distributes the workload in the kitchen.

_____

_____

T   F   4.   The ultimate goal of menu mix is a combination of items that generate the most sales at the lowest prices.

_____

_____

T   F   5.   The "going rate" is the price that competitors are charging for menu items.

_____

_____

T   F   6.   Competent operators base their menu price on the going rate of menu items.

_____

_____

(Continued)

Activity B *(Continued)*   **Name** _____

T   F   7.   The simplest cost-based pricing method is the food cost percentage method.

_____

_____

T   F   8.   The markup method involves adding a set amount to the cost of the menu item.

_____

_____

Basing Price on Standard Food Cost Percentage

Chapter 50

Activity C

Name _____

Date _____ Period _____

Foodservice operations commonly use the standard food cost percentage method to set menu prices. Use the following formula to complete the chart and answer the questions that follow. (Round answers up to nearest 25 cents, for example $6.02 rounds up to $6.25; $6.42 rounds up to $6.50; $6.80 rounds up to $7.00.)

Food cost per portion ÷ Standard food cost percentage = Menu price

Example: The manager of an operation that has established a 30% standard food cost needs to set a menu price for an appetizer portion of spring rolls. The recipe cost sheet performed on an appetizer portion of spring rolls shows a food cost per portion of $1.96.

Step 1. First convert the standard food cost percent to a decimal by moving the decimal point two places to the left.

$$30\% = .30.0 = 0.30$$

Step 2. Calculate the menu price using the formula.

Food cost per portion ÷ Standard food cost percentage = Menu price

$$\$1.96 ÷ 0.30 = \$6.53 = \text{(round up)} \ \$6.75$$

Food Item	Food Cost per Portion	Standard Food Cost Percentage	Menu Price
Green salad	$1.23	35%	
Lentil soup	$0.80	30%	
Beef entrée	$4.05	36%	
Fruit compote dessert	$1.67	32%	

1. If the restaurant above increased their standard food cost percentage to 32%, what would the new menu price for the lentil soup be?

_____

2. If the same restaurant lowered their standard food cost percentage to 28%, what would the new menu price for the lentil soup be?

_____

3. If a restaurant raises their standard food cost percentage, the menu price will (**increase**) (**decrease**) (**stay the same**).

4. If a restaurant lowers their standard food cost percentage, the menu price will (**increase**) (**decrease**) (**stay the same**).

Menu Mechanics

Chapter 50

Activity D

Name _____

Date _____Period_____

Part 1

Circle the clue in parentheses that best completes each of the following statements.

1. Menu text should be accurate and (**colorful**) (**truthful**).

2. Menu text should be descriptive and as (**detailed**) (**brief**) as possible.

3. Menu text should avoid (**home-cooking terms**) (**culinary jargon**).

4. Menu text should be written in a language (**that will most impress customers**) (**with which customers are most familiar**).

5. Menu text should include the portion size of the main (**protein**) (**starch**) (**carbohydrate**) source.

6. Menu text should describe the (**finished look of the product**) (**cooking method**).

7. Menu text should highlight (**difficult processes**) (**unique ingredients**) that make the dish special.

Part 2

Complete the following list of elements to consider when planning menu design and layout.

8. Size, shape, and color of the menu card.

9. _____

10. _____

11. _____

12. _____

13. _____

Developing Taste

Culinary Terminology

Chapter 51

Activity A

Name _____

Date _____ Period _____

Below is a professional chef's reply to a student considering a culinary career. Fill in each blank with the appropriate term from Chapter 51. For each term, underline the words in the letter that define that term.

Dear Culinary Hopeful:

You asked about the skills that chefs must develop. Well, of course there are many, and one that you may not have considered is 1._____, the sense of taste. Did you know that taste involves your nose as well as your mouth? 2._____ , or your sense of smell, interprets airborne molecules that enter the nasal cavity and come in contact with the olfactory bulb. The signals travel from the olfactory bulb to the brain for interpretation as "taste." So the nose is important, but it's not the only passage to the olfactory bulb! When you swallow, aromas are propelled from the back of your throat up the back of your nasal cavity. This indirect route to the nasal cavity and, ultimately, the olfactory bulb is called the 3. _____.

Mouths can actually perceive only five basic tastes. You are probably aware of the basic tastes of sweet, salty, sour, and bitter. There is one more basic taste that Western cultures are just beginning to understand. This taste, called 4. _____, results from a type of protein called a glutamate. It is especially noticeable in fermented soy products, certain ripe vegetables, mushrooms, sea vegetables, aged cheeses, and monosodium glutamate.

Although the mouth can distinguish between only five basic tastes, it can also register the sense of touch. When you chew, the inside of your mouth registers texture. That ability is what allows you to gauge whether a steak is tender or tough. The same ability allows you to perceive 5. _____, or the spicy hot sensation that is part of some dishes. Foods with chiles, peppercorns, onions, garlic, and mustard produce this sensation.

Developing your sense of taste takes work, but it is well worth the effort. I consider my sense of taste to be the most powerful tool I have for maintaining quality control in the kitchen.

Master Chef

Reviewing Key Concepts

Chapter 51

Activity B

Name _____

Date _____ Period _____

Circle the clue in parentheses that best completes each of the following statements.

1. The general process of ingesting food is referred to as (**eating**) (**tasting**).

2. (**Eating**) (**Tasting**) requires more concentration than (**eating**) (**tasting**).

3. (**Eating**) (**Tasting**) is the process of thoughtfully analyzing foods and beverages using your senses.

4. Genetic makeup is a (**subjective**) (**physical**) factor that affects taste.

5. Age is a (**subjective**) (**physical**) factor that affects taste.

6. Head trauma and certain medical treatments can be a (**subjective**) (**physical**) factor that affects taste.

7. Memory is a (**subjective**) (**physical**) factor that affects taste.

8. Some medicines are a (**subjective**) (**physical**) factor that affects taste.

9. Culture is a (**subjective**) (**physical**) factor that affects taste.

10. The transmission of aroma molecules to the nasal cavity and olfactory bulb are examples of how the sense of (**smell**) (**taste**) (**touch**) helps our bodies perceive taste.

11. The 10,000 taste buds on the papillae of the tongue are examples of how the sense of (**smell**) (**taste**) (**touch**) helps our bodies perceive taste.

12. The perceived tastes of sweet, salty, sour, bitter, and umami are examples of how the sense of (**smell**) (**taste**) (**touch**) helps our bodies perceive taste.

13. The ability to perceive mustard, chiles, peppercorns, and other piquant ingredients is an example of how the sense of (**smell**) (**taste**) (**touch**) helps our bodies perceive taste.

14. In addition to piquant, the mouth also perceives differences in (**temperature**) (**texture**) (**temperature and texture**).

Taste Combinations

Chapter 51

Activity C

Name _____

Date _____ Period _____

Part 1

Match the following foods to the taste or sensation they contribute to a dish. Some foods may contribute more than one taste or sensation.

_____ 1. Chocolate

_____ 2. Citrus juice

_____ 3. Coffee

_____ 4. Honey

_____ 5. Molasses

_____ 6. Mushrooms

_____ 7. Mustard

_____ 8. Seaweed

_____ 9. Sugar

_____ 10. Tomato

_____ 11. Vinegar

A. acid

B. bitter

C. piquant

D. salty

E. sweet

F. umami

Part 2

Complete the basic taste pairings below.

12. Sweet and _____

13. Sweet and _____

14. Sweet and _____

15. Fat and _____

16. Salt and _____

Notes